□ Indiana

interactive SCIENCE

This bird is brown all winter. Then, during the mating season, male American goldfinches replace brown feathers with bright yellow feathers.

PEARSON

Glenview, Illinois • Boston, Massachusetts • Chandler, Arizona • Upper Saddle River, New Jersey

Authors

You are an author!

You are one of the authors of this book. You can write in this book! You can take notes in this book! You can draw in it too! This book will be yours to keep.

Fill in the information below to tell about yourself. Then write your autobiography. An autobiography tells about you and the kinds of things you like to do.

My Photo

Name
....

School
....

Town, State
....

Autobiography
....

....

....

....

....

....

....

....

....

On The Cover
This bird is brown all winter. Then, during the mating season, male American goldfinches replace brown feathers with bright yellow feathers.

PEARSON

ISBN-13:   978-0-328-52092-3
ISBN-10:   0-328-52092-6
1 2 3 4 5 6 7 8 9 10 V042 19 18 17 16 15 14 13 12 11 10

Program Authors

DON BUCKLEY, M.Sc.
*Information and Communications Technology Director,
The School at Columbia University, New York, New York*
Mr. Buckley has been at the forefront of K–12 educational
technology for nearly two decades. A founder of New York City
Independent School Technologists (NYCIST) and long-time chair
of New York Association of Independent Schools' annual IT
conference, he has taught students on two continents and
created multimedia and Internet-based instructional systems
for schools worldwide.

ZIPPORAH MILLER, M.A.Ed.
*Associate Executive Director for Professional Programs
and Conferences, National Science Teachers Association,
Arlington, Virginia*
Associate executive director for professional programs and
conferences at NSTA, Ms. Zipporah Miller is a former K–12 science
supervisor and STEM coordinator for the Prince George's County
Public School District in Maryland. She is a science education
consultant who has overseen curriculum development and staff
training for more than 150 district science coordinators.

MICHAEL J. PADILLA, Ph.D.
*Associate Dean and Director, Eugene P. Moore School of
Education, Clemson University, Clemson, South Carolina*
A former middle school teacher and a leader in middle school science
education, Dr. Michael Padilla has served as president of the National
Science Teachers Association and as a writer of the National Science
Education Standards. He is professor of science education at Clemson
University. As lead author of the *Science Explorer* series, Dr. Padilla
has inspired the team in developing a program that promotes student
inquiry and meets the needs of today's students.

KATHRYN THORNTON, Ph.D.
*Professor and Associate Dean, School of Engineering
and Applied Science, University of Virginia,
Charlottesville, Virginia*
Selected by NASA in May 1984, Dr. Kathryn Thornton is a veteran
of four space flights. She has logged more than 975 hours in space,
including more than 21 hours of extravehicular activity. As an
author on the *Scott Foresman Science* series, Dr. Thornton's
enthusiasm for science has inspired teachers around the globe.

MICHAEL E. WYSESSION, Ph.D.
*Associate Professor of Earth and Planetary Science,
Washington University, St. Louis, Missouri*
An author on more than 50 scientific publications, Dr. Wysession
was awarded the prestigious Packard Foundation Fellowship and
Presidential Faculty Fellowship for his research in geophysics. Dr.
Wysession is an expert on Earth's inner structure and has mapped
various regions of Earth using seismic tomography. He is known
internationally for his work in geoscience education and outreach.

Understanding by Design® Author

GRANT WIGGINS, Ed.D.
*President, Authentic Education,
Hopewell, New Jersey*
Dr. Wiggins is coauthor of *Understanding
by Design®* (UbD), a philosophy of
instructional design. UbD is a disciplined
way of thinking about curriculum design,
assessment, and instruction that moves
teaching from content to understanding.

Planet Diary Author

JACK HANKIN
*Science/Mathematics Teacher,
The Hilldale School, Daly City, California
Founder, Planet Diary Web site*
Mr. Hankin is the creator and writer
of Planet Diary, a science current events
Web site. Mr. Hankin is passionate about
bringing science news and environmental
awareness into classrooms.

Activities Author

KAREN L. OSTLUND, Ph.D.
*Advisory Council, Texas Natural Science
Center, College of Natural Sciences,
The University of Texas at Austin*
Dr. Ostlund has more than 35 years of
experience teaching at the elementary,
middle school, and university levels.
Previously Dr. Ostlund served as the Director
of WINGS Online (Welcoming Interns and
Novices with Guidance and Support) and
the Director of the UTeach | Dell Center
for New Teacher Success with the UTeach
program in the College of Natural Sciences
at the University of Texas at Austin. She
also served as the Director of the Center for
Science Education at the University of Texas
at Arlington, President of the Council of
Elementary Science International, and on the
Board of Directors of the National Science
Teachers Association. As an author of the
Scott Foresman Science series, Dr. Ostlund
was instrumental in developing inquiry
activities.

ELL Consultant

JIM CUMMINS, Ph.D.
*Professor and Canada Research Chair,
Curriculum, Teaching and Learning
Department at the University of Toronto*
Dr. Cummins's research focuses on literacy
development in multilingual schools and the
role technology plays in learning across the
curriculum. *Interactive Science* incorporates
research-based principles for integrating
language with the teaching of academic
content based on Dr. Cummins's work.

Reviewers

Program Consultants

WILLIAM BROZO, Ph.D.
Professor of Literacy, Graduate School of Education, George Mason University, Fairfax, Virginia.
Dr. Brozo is the author of numerous articles and books on literacy development. He co-authors a column in The Reading Teacher and serves on the editorial review board of the Journal of Adolescent & Adult Literacy.

KRISTI ZENCHAK, M.S.
Biology Instructor, Oakton Community College, Des Plaines, Illinois
Kristi Zenchak helps elementary teachers incorporate science, technology, engineering, and math activities into the classroom. STEM activities that produce viable solutions to real-world problems not only motivate students but also prepare students for future STEM careers. Ms. Zenchak helps elementary teachers understand the basic science concepts, and provides STEM activities that are easy to implement in the classroom.

Content Reviewers

Paul Beale, Ph.D.
Department of Physics
University of Colorado
Boulder, Colorado

Joy Branlund, Ph.D.
Department of Earth Science
Southwestern Illinois College
Granite City, Illinois

Constance Brown, Ph.D
Atmospheric Science Program
Geography Department
Indiana University
Bloomington, Indiana

Dana Dudle, Ph.D.
Biology Department
DePauw University
Greencastle, Indiana

Rick Duhrkopf, Ph. D.
Department of Biology
Baylor University
Waco, Texas

Mark Henriksen, Ph.D.
Physics Department
University of Maryland
Baltimore, Maryland

Andrew Hirsch, Ph.D.
Department of Physics
Purdue University
W. Lafayette, Indiana

Linda L. Cronin Jones, Ph.D.
School of Teaching & Learning
University of Florida
Gainesville, Florida

T. Griffith Jones, Ph.D.
College of Education
University of Florida
Gainesville, Florida

Candace Lutzow-Felling, Ph.D.
Director of Education
State Arboretum of Virginia &
    Blandy Experimental Farm
Boyce VA 22620

Cortney V. Martin, Ph.D.
Virginia Polytechnic Institute
Blacksburg, Virginia

Sadredin Moosavi, Ph.D.
University of Massachusetts
    Dartmouth
Fairhaven, Massachusetts

Klaus Newmann, Ph.D.
Department of Geological
    Sciences
Ball State University
Muncie, Indiana

Scott M. Rochette, Ph.D.
Department of the Earth
    Sciences
SUNY College at Brockport
Brockport, New York

Karyn Rogers, Ph.D.
Department of Geological
    Sciences
University of Missouri
Columbia, Missouri

Laurence Rosenhein, Ph.D.
Dept. of Chemistry and Physics
Indiana State University
Terre Haute, Indiana

Sara Seager, Ph.D.
Department of Planetary Science
    and Physics
Massachusetts Institute of
    Technology
Cambridge, MA 02139

William H. Steinecker. Ph.D.
Research Scholar
Miami University
Oxford, Ohio

Paul R. Stoddard, Ph.D.
Department of Geology and
    Environmental Geosciences
Northern Illinois University
DeKalb, Illinois

Laurence Rosenhein, Ph. D.
Department of Chemistry
Indiana State University
Terre Haute, Indiana

Janet Vaglia, Ph. D.
Department of Biology
DePauw University
Greencastle, Indiana

Ed Zalisko, Ph.D.
Professor of Biology
Blackburn College
Carlinville, Illinois

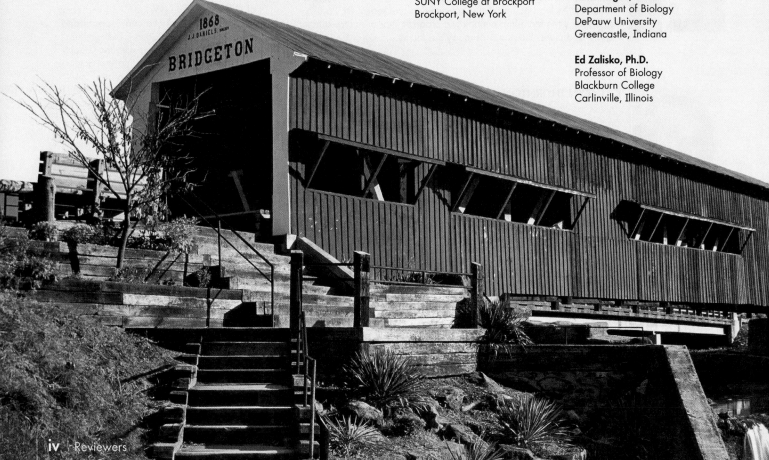

Built especially for Indiana

Indiana *Interactive Science* covers 100% of Indiana's Academic Standards for Science without extraneous content. Built on feedback from Indiana educators, *Interactive Science* focuses on what is important to Indiana teachers and students, creating a personal, relevant, and engaging classroom experience.

Indiana K-8 Science Teacher Advisory Board

Jodi Allen
Glen Acres Elementary School
Lafayette, IN

Rick Dubbs
Monrovia Middle School
Monrovia, IN

Margaret Flack
Vincennes University
    Jasper Campus
Jasper, IN

Michael Gibson
New Haven Middle School
New Haven, IN

Jill Hatcher
Spring Mill Elementary School
Indianapolis, IN

Jamie Hooten
Lincoln Elementary School
Bedford, IN

Jamil Odom
Mary Bryan Elementary School
Indianapolis, IN

Mike Robards
Franklin Community Middle School
Franklin, IN

Richard Towle
Noblesville Middle School
Noblesville, IN

K-8 National Master Teacher Board

Tricia Burke
E. F. Young Elementary School
Chicago, IL

Lisa Catandella
Brentwood UFSD
Brentwood, NY

Karen Clements
Lynch Elementary School
Winchester, MA

Emily Compton
Park Forest Middle School
Baton Rouge, LA

Pansy Cowder
Lincoln Magnet School
Plant City, FL

Georgi Delgadillo
East Valley School District
Spokane, WA

Dr. Rick Fairman
McGregor School of Education
Antioch University
Yellow Springs, OH

Joe Fescatore
Green Elementary School
La Mesa, CA

Mimi Halferty
Gorzycki Middle School
Austin, TX

Christy Herring
Prairie Trace Elementary School
Carmel, IN

Treva Jeffries
Toledo Public Schools
Toledo, OH

James Kuhl
Central Square Middle School
Central Square, NY

Dr. Patsy Latin
Caddo Public School District
Shreveport, LA

Greg Londot
Hidden Hills Elementary School
Phoenix, AZ

Stan Melby
Sheridan Road Elementary
Fort Sill, OK

Bonnie Mizell
Howard Middle School
Orlando, FL

Dr. Joel Palmer
Mesquite ISD
Mesquite, TX

Leslie Pohley
Largo Middle School
Largo, FL

Susan Pritchard
Washington Middle School
La Habra, CA

Anne Rice
Woodland Middle School
Gurnee, IL

Adrienne Sawyer
Chesapeake Public Schools
Chesapeake, VA

Richard Towle
Noblesville Middle School
Noblesville, IN

Dr. Madhu Uppal
Schaumburg School District
Schaumburg, IL

Maria Valdez
Mark Twain Elementary School
Wheeling, IL

Viv Wayne
Montgomery County Public Schools
Rockville, MD

Indiana Unit A
Science, Engineering, and Technology

The Nature of Science

Scientists use satellite data to track storms.

O **myscienceonline.com**

Untamed Science™
Watch the Ecogeeks and
learn about the nature
of science.

Got it? ⏱ **60-Second Video**
Take a minute to learn about
the nature of science.

I Will Know...
See what you've learned
about the nature of science.

Investigate It! Virtual Lab
Do your experiment online!

Memory Match
Practice vocabulary with an
interactive matching game.

Technology and the Design Process

Computers are used by people all over the world.

MYSCIENCEONLINE.com

Untamed Science™
Get the answers to questions about technology and the design process from the Ecogeeks.

Got it? 60-Second Video
Take a minute to learn about technology and the design process.

Envision It!
See what you already know about technology and the design process.

Explore It! Animation
Watch your lab online!

MY PLANET DIARY
Learn about the discovery of microwaves.

Matter and Its Properties

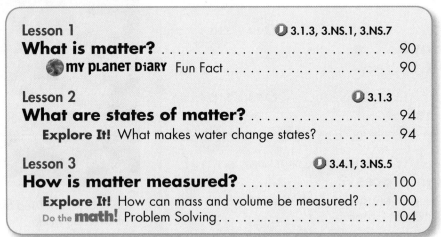

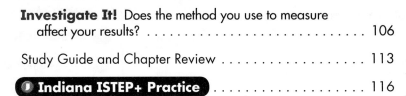

Length is one property of matter that can be measured.

❶ mYscienceonLine.com

🦎 Untamed Science™
Watch the Ecogeeks as they learn about matter and its properties.

Got *it*? ⏱ 60-Second Video
Take a minute to learn about matter and its properties.

▶ **Explore It!** Animation
Go online to watch this experiment about matter and its properties!

🌎 mY pLaneT DiaRY
Learn fun facts about matter and its properties.

Envision It!
See what you already know about matter and its properties.

Indiana

Chapter 4

Indiana Unit B Summary

Forms of Energy

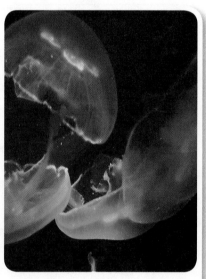

Light can pass through these sea jellies.

● **myscienceonline.com**

Untamed Science™
The Ecogeeks answer your questions about forms of energy.

Got it? 60-Second Video
Take a minute to learn about forms of energy.

? I Will Know...
A fun way to review what you've learned about forms of energy

Investigate It! Simulation
Try this lab online!

Memory Match
Practice vocabulary with an interactive matching game.

Indiana

Chapter 5

Minerals and Rocks

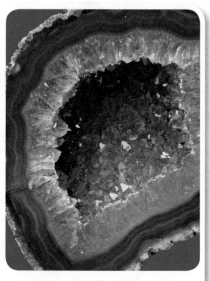

Agate is found in many places around the world.

❶ **my**science**online.com**

🐾 **Untamed Science**
Get answers to questions about minerals and rocks from the Ecogeeks.

Got *it?* ⏱ **60-Second Video**
Review each lesson about minerals and rocks in 60 seconds!

❓ **I Will Know...**
A fun way to see what you've learned about minerals and rocks

Envision It!
See what you already know about minerals and rocks

Investigate It! Virtual Lab
Interact with the lab and see what happens!

Indiana Unit D
Life Science

Plants

Peonies, Indiana's state flower, need sunlight and water to grow.

🌐 **myscienceonline.com**

🦎 **UntamedScience™**
Watch the Ecogeeks learn about plants.

Got it? ⏱ **60-Second Video**
Review what you learned about plants in 60 seconds.

Explore It! Animation
Watch your lab online!

🌍 **my PLANET DIARY**
Learn fun and interesting science facts about plants.

Vocabulary Smart Cards
Mix and match vocabulary practice

"This is your book. You can write in it!"

interactive SCIENCE

Big Question

At the start of each chapter you will see two questions—an **Engaging Question** and a **Big Question.** Just like a scientist, you will predict an answer to the Engaging Question. Each Big Question will help you start thinking about Indiana's Big Ideas of science. Look for the ? symbol throughout the chapter!

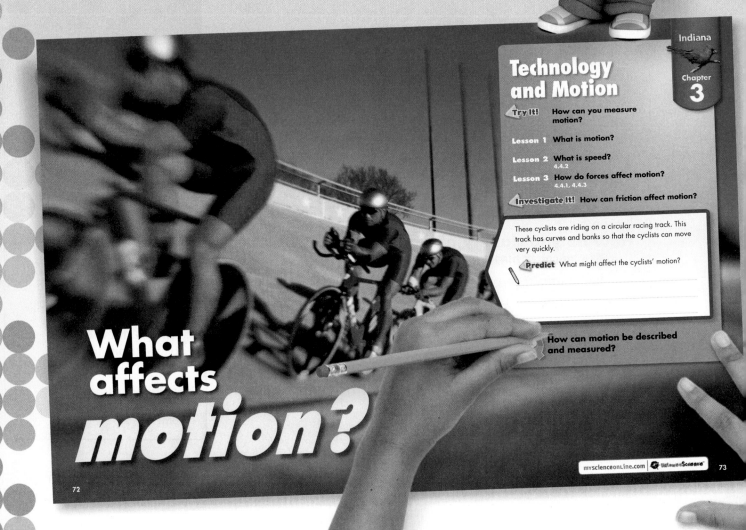

What affects motion?

Indiana

Chapter 3

Technology and Motion

Try It! How can you measure motion?

Lesson 1 What is motion?

Lesson 2 What is speed?
4.4.2

Lesson 3 How do forces affect motion?
4.4.1, 4.4.3

Investigate It! How can friction affect motion?

These cyclists are riding on a circular racing track. This track has curves and banks so that the cyclists can move very quickly.

Predict What might affect the cyclists' motion?
_____
_____

How can motion be described and measured?

mysciencecnline.com

Let's Read Science!

You will see a page like this toward the beginning of each chapter. It will show you how to use a reading skill that will help you understand what you read.

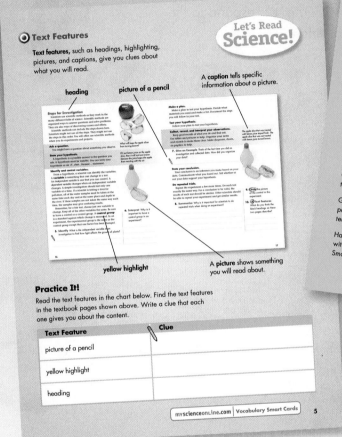

Practice It!

Read the text features in the chart below. Find the text features in the textbook pages shown above. Write a clue that each one gives you about the content.

Text Feature	Clue
picture of a pencil	
yellow highlight	
heading	

myscienceonline.com | Vocabulary Smart Cards | 5

Vocabulary Smart Cards

Go to the end of the chapter and cut out your own set of **Vocabulary Smart Cards.** Write a sentence, draw a picture, or use a vocabulary strategy to learn the word. Play a game with a classmate to practice using the word!

myscienceonline.com | Untamed Science™

Look for **MyScienceOnline.com** technology options.
At MyScienceOnline.com you can immerse yourself in virtual environments, get extra practice, and even blog about current events in science.

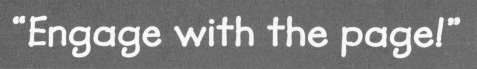

"Engage with the page!"

interactive SCIENCE

Envision It!

At the beginning of each lesson, at the top of the page, you will see an **Envision It!** interactivity that gives you the opportunity to circle, draw, write, or respond to the Envision It! question.

Lesson 4

How do organisms get and use energy?

Observe and classify common Indiana organisms as producers, consumers, decomposers, predator and prey based on their relationships and interactions with other organisms in their ecosystem. (Also ...)

Envision It!

Tell how you think plants get the energy they need to live.

I will know how plants use energy from the sun.

Words to Know

photosynthesis
cellular respiration

MY PLANET DIARY for Indiana

DISCOVERY

What comes to mind when you think of corn? You might think of corn on the cob, popcorn, or cornbread. However, corn is not just food. Scientists have discovered that it can also be used to produce a liquid fuel called ethanol. Ethanol is a type of biofuel. Biofuels are fuels made from living things. Other plants used to make biofuel are soy and sugarcane. Biofuels are more environmentally friendly than other fuels, such as gasoline. Because gasoline-powered vehicles produce air pollution, using biofuels instead might help preserve Earth's environment.

How do you think biofuels might affect your life?

myscienceonline.com | My planet diary | 254

Energy Sources

What is your favorite type of green salad? You might like one made of spinach. Perhaps you choose iceberg lettuce or crispy romaine lettuce. Spinach, iceberg lettuce, and romaine lettuce are all types of leaves. A leaf is a major plant part. Unlike animals, plants make their own food. Most of the food that a plant makes is made in the plant's leaves.

When you eat spinach or lettuce leaves, your body gets their energy. Your body cells need this energy to carry out its many functions. The energy you get is stored in the leaves. Where did the leaves get this energy? It came from the sun in the form of sunlight. The sun is Earth's primary energy source. The plant used the sunlight's energy to make its food, which it uses to grow. This form of energy passes on to you when you eat the leaves.

1. Identify Where does the stored energy in these cabbage leaves come from?

cabbage

2. Explain How does a plant get its food?

myscienceonline.com | Envision It! | 255

MY PLANET DIARY

My Planet Diary interactivities will introduce you to amazing scientists, fun facts, and important discoveries in science. They will also help you to overcome common misconceptions about science concepts.

After reading small chunks of information, stop to check your understanding. The visuals help teach about what you read. Answer questions, underline text, draw pictures, or label models.

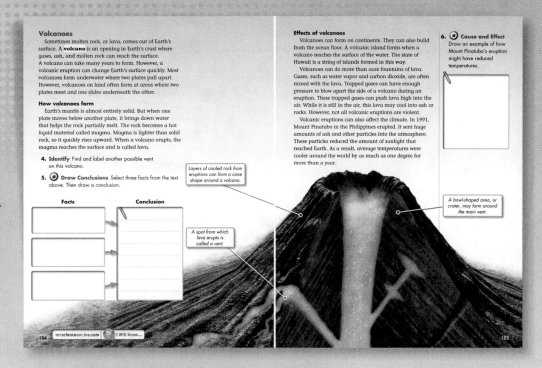

Volcanoes

Sometimes molten rock, or lava, comes out of Earth's surface. A **volcano** is an opening in Earth's crust where gases, ash, and molten rock can reach the surface. A volcano can take many years to form. However, a volcanic eruption can change Earth's surface quickly. Most volcanoes form underwater where two plates pull apart. However, volcanoes on land often form at areas where two plates meet and one slides underneath the other.

How volcanoes form

Earth's mantle is almost entirely solid. But when one plate moves below another plate, it brings down water that helps the rock partially melt. The rock becomes a hot liquid material called magma. Magma is lighter than solid rock, so it quickly rises upward. When a volcano erupts, the magma reaches the surface and is called lava.

4. Identify Find and label another possible vent on this volcano.

5. ⊙ Draw Conclusions Select three facts from the text above. Then draw a conclusion.

Facts	Conclusion

Layers of cooled rock from eruptions can form a cone shape around a volcano.

A spot from which lava erupts is called a vent.

A bowl-shaped area, or crater, may form around the main vent.

Effects of volcanoes

Volcanoes can form on continents. They can also build from the ocean floor. A volcanic island forms when a volcano reaches the surface of the water. The state of Hawaii is a string of islands formed in this way.

Volcanoes can do more than ooze fountains of lava. Gases, such as water vapor and carbon dioxide, are often mixed with the lava. Trapped gases can have enough pressure to blow apart the side of a volcano during an eruption. These trapped gases can push lava high into the air. While it is still in the air, this lava may cool into ash or rocks. However, not all volcanic eruptions are violent.

Volcanic eruptions can also affect the climate. In 1991, Mount Pinatubo in the Philippines erupted. It sent huge amounts of ash and other particles into the atmosphere. These particles reduced the amount of sunlight that reached Earth. As a result, average temperatures were cooler around the world by as much as one degree for more than a year.

6. ⊙ Cause and Effect Draw an example of how Mount Pinatubo's eruption might have reduced temperatures.

184   mYscienceonline.com   I Will Know...   185

Velocity and Acceleration

Some objects change speed *and direction.* **Velocity** is both the speed and the direction an object is moving. Some words that describe direction are *north, south, east,* and *west.* Others are *left, right, up,* and *down.*

Any change in the speed or direction of an object's motion is acceleration. Starting, speeding up, and slowing down are accelerations. The roller coaster accelerates as it speeds up or slows down. It is changing speed. A roller coaster on a curved path accelerates even if its speed does not change. That is because it changes direction as it moves around the curve.

7. Decide Which of the following is NOT an example of an acceleration?
   a. An airplane moving at the same speed in the same direction
   b. An airplane slowing its speed and moving down to land
   c. An airplane slowing its speed and moving in the same direction

8. Summarize What are two things that must be measured in order to find an object's velocity?

9. Illustrate Look at the roller coaster on the opposite page. Draw a solid arrow where the roller coaster slows down, and a dotted arrow where the coaster speeds up.

10. ⊙ Sequence First, the roller coaster slows as it moves up to the top of the loop. Write what happens next.

Got it? ⊙ 4.4.2

11. Produce How do you calculate average speed?

12. ⊙ Distinguish What is the difference between speed and velocity?

☐ **Stop!** I need help with

❚❚ **Wait!** I have a question about

▶ **Go!** Now I know

Do the math!

Calculate Percentages

Race cars travel quickly around racetracks. To determine how much of the track has been traveled, fill in the chart by finding the fraction, decimal, and percentage. The first row is done for you.

Amount of Track Traveled		
Fraction	**Decimal**	**Percentage**
$\frac{80}{100}$	0.80	80%
$\frac{50}{100}$	0.50	
$\frac{35}{100}$		
	0.25	25%

86   mYscienceonline.com   Got it?   60-Second Video

mYscienceonline.com   Got it? Quiz   87

Scientists commonly use math as a tool to help them answer science questions. You can practice skills that you are learning in math class right in your Interactive Science Student Edition!

At the end of each lesson you will have a chance to evaluate your own progress! After answering the **Got it?** questions, think about how you are doing. At this point you can stop, wait, or go on to the next lesson.

"Have fun! Be a scientist!"

interactive SCIENCE

▶ Try It!

At the start of every chapter, you will have the chance to do a hands-on inquiry lab. The lab will provide you with experiences that will prepare you for the chapter lessons or may raise a new question in your mind.

▶ Explore It!

Before you start reading the lesson, **Explore It!** activities provide you with an opportunity to first explore the content!

Design It!

The **Design It!** activity has you use the engineering design process to find solutions to problems. By identifying the problem, doing research, and developing possible solutions, you will design, construct, and test a prototype for a real world problem. Communicate your evidence through graphs, tables, drawings, and prototypes and identify ways to make your solution better.

STEM activities are found throughout core and ancillary materials.

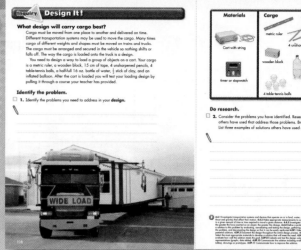

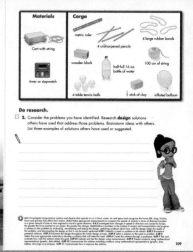

Investigate It!

At the end of every chapter, a Directed Inquiry lab gives you a chance to put together everything you've learned in the chapter. Using the activity card, apply design principles in the Guided version to Modify Your Investigation or the Open version to Develop Your Own Investigation. Whether you need a lot of support from your teacher or you're ready to explore on your own, there are fun hands-on activities that match your interests.

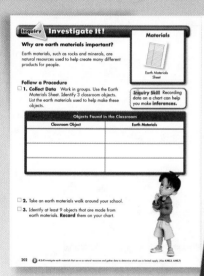

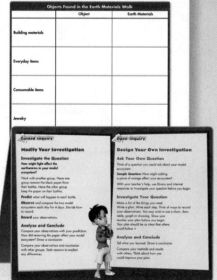

Apply It!

At the end of every unit, an Open Inquiry lab gives you a chance to explore science using scientific methods.

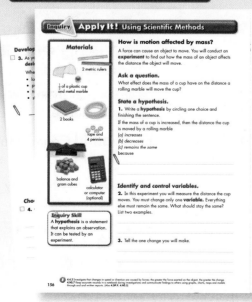

"Go online anytime!"

interactive SCIENCE

Here's how you log in...

1 Go to www.myscienceonline.com.

2 Log in with your username and password.

Username: _____

Password: _____

3 Click on your program and select your chapter.

Check it out!

Watch a Video!

 Untamed Science Join the Ecogeeks on their video adventure.

Got it? 60-Second Video Review each lesson in 60 seconds.

Go Digital for Inquiry!

Explore It! Simulation Watch the lab online.

Investigate It! Virtual Lab Do the lab online.

Show What You Know!

Got it? Quiz Take a quick quiz and get instant feedback.

ISTEP+ Practice Prepare for the "big test."

Writing for Science Write to help you unlock the Big Question.

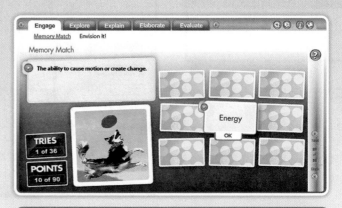

Get Excited About Science!

The Big Question Share what you think about the Big Question.

my planet Diary Connect to the world of science.

Envision It! Connect to what you already know before you start each lesson.

Memory Match Play a game to build your vocabulary.

Get Help!

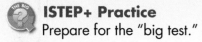 **my science COACH** Get help at your level.

Science, Engineering, and Technology

Chapter 1

The Nature of Science

What is science?

Chapter 2

Technology and the Design Process

How can technology affect our lives?

What can you ask about lake water?

The Nature of Science

 Try It! Why is it important to communicate clearly?

Investigate It! How does a microscope make your observations easier?

These student scientists are studying the quality of lake water. They are using tools and recording their observations. They could analyze their data in the boat or back at school.

 Predict What type of observations about water do you think they are making?

....

....

What is science?

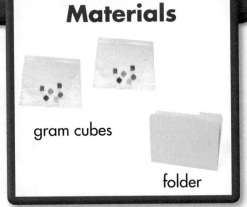

Inquiry ▶ Try It!

Why is it important to communicate clearly?

☑ **1.** Work with a partner. Take 6 cubes each. Set up a folder so that you cannot see each other's work.

☑ **2.** **Design** and build a simple structure.

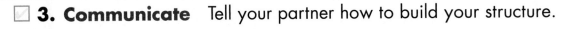

Materials

gram cubes

folder

> **Inquiry Skill**
> Scientists **communicate** when they explain how to do something.

☑ **3.** **Communicate**   Tell your partner how to build your structure.

☑ **4.** Take the folder down. Compare the structures.

☑ **5.** Trade jobs and repeat.

Explain Your Results

6. **UNLOCK THE BIG ?** Think about the words you used in **communicating** your **design** to your partner. List the words that were most helpful in communicating clearly.

....

7. Why was it important to communicate clearly with your partner? **Infer** why it is important for scientists to communicate clearly with one another.

....

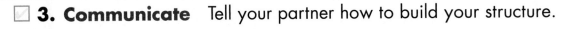

3.NS.3 Plan and carry out investigations as a class, in small groups or independently, often over a period of several class lessons. (Also **3.DP.4**)

Text Features

Text features, such as headings, highlighting, pictures, and captions, give you clues about what you will read.

A **heading** tells what the content that follows is about.

A **picture** shows something you will read about.

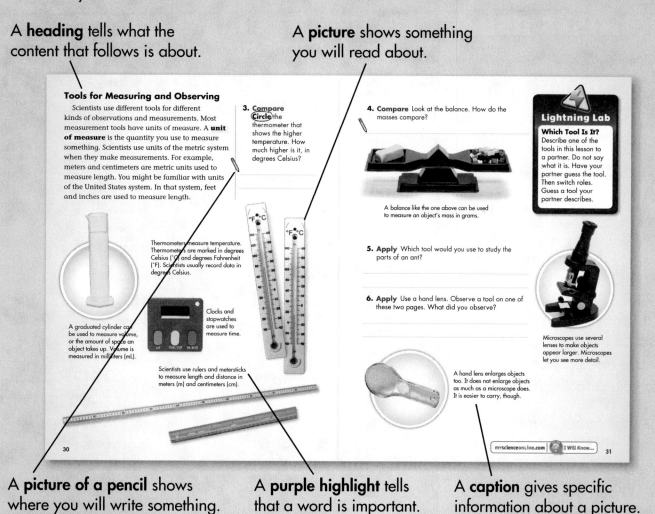

Tools for Measuring and Observing

Scientists use different tools for different kinds of observations and measurements. Most measurement tools have units of measure. A **unit of measure** is the quantity you use to measure something. Scientists use units of the metric system when they make measurements. For example, meters and centimeters are metric units used to measure length. You might be familiar with units of the United States system. In that system, feet and inches are used to measure length.

A graduated cylinder can be used to measure volume, or the amount of space an object takes up. Volume is measured in milliliters (mL).

Thermometers measure temperature. Thermometers are marked in degrees Celsius (°C) and degrees Fahrenheit (°F). Scientists usually record data in degrees Celsius.

Clocks and stopwatches are used to measure time.

Scientists use rulers and metersticks to measure length and distance in meters (m) and centimeters (cm).

3. **Compare** Circle the thermometer that shows the higher temperature. How much higher is it, in degrees Celsius?

4. **Compare** Look at the balance. How do the masses compare?

A balance like the one above can be used to measure an object's mass in grams.

5. **Apply** Which tool would you use to study the parts of an ant?

6. **Apply** Use a hand lens. Observe a tool on one of these two pages. What did you observe?

A hand lens enlarges objects too. It does not enlarge objects as much as a microscope does. It is easier to carry, though.

Lightning Lab

Which Tool Is It?
Describe one of the tools in this lesson to a partner. Do not say what it is. Have your partner guess the tool. Then switch roles. Guess a tool your partner describes.

Microscopes use several lenses to make objects appear larger. Microscopes let you see more detail.

30

31

myscienceonline.com | I Will Know...

A **picture of a pencil** shows where you will write something.

A **purple highlight** tells that a word is important.

A **caption** gives specific information about a picture.

Practice It!

Read the text features in the chart below. Write a clue that each one gives you about the content.

Text feature	Clue
picture	
caption	
heading	

What questions do scientists ask?

3.NS.1 Make predictions and formulate testable questions. 3.NS.2 Design a fair test. (Also 3.NS.3)

Envision It!

Tell a question that a scientist could ask about these orange trees.

my planet Diary

Have you ever heard of moon trees? Moon trees do not come from the moon. They are trees grown from seeds taken to the moon.

NASA astronaut Stuart Roosa took seeds to the moon on the Apollo 14 mission in 1971. When he brought the seeds back to Earth, NASA scientists examined them. Scientists wanted to learn if space travel changed the seeds. Then they planted the seeds. No one knew what the trees would look like or if the seeds would grow.

As the seeds grew, NASA scientists made observations. These observations helped scientists learn how space travel affects seed growth.

DISCOVERY

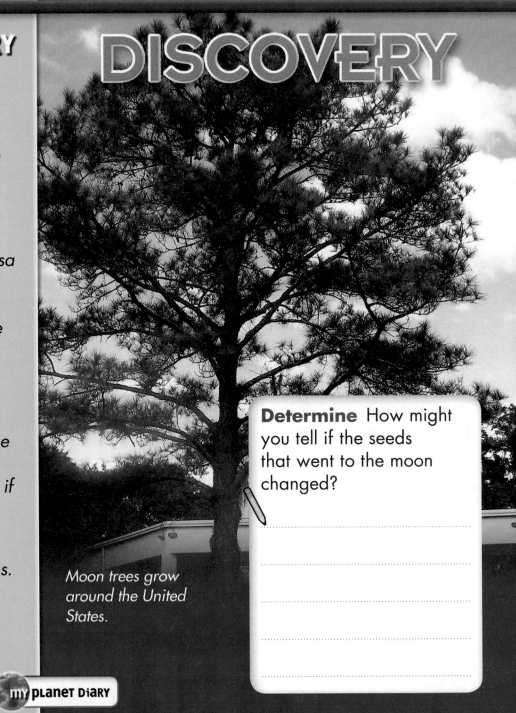

Moon trees grow around the United States.

Determine How might you tell if the seeds that went to the moon changed?

....
....
....
....
....

myscienceonline.com | my planet Diary

Words to Know

scientist   inquiry
investigate

Scientists

What type of soil works best to grow corn and soybeans? That is a question a scientist might ask. A **scientist** is a person who asks questions about the natural world. Scientists collect observations in an organized way to investigate their questions. To **investigate** means to look for answers. Then scientists explain their answers.

Everyone can be a scientist. You are a scientist when you ask questions and investigate. What questions do you ask about the natural world?

1. ◎ **Text Features** Look at the text features on this page. Identify two text features and the clues they give you.

Text feature	Clue

This scientist is studying crop fertilizers. He might ask a question about what kind of fertilizer will help plants grow the largest.

Questions

Science begins with inquiry. **Inquiry** means the process of asking questions. Scientists ask questions that they can investigate. The questions might come from something scientists observe or a problem they know. What type of soil works best to grow corn and soybeans? How can I grow bigger crops? How can I keep insects from eating crops? These are some questions scientists might ask.

Questions That Science Cannot Answer

Some questions cannot be answered by investigating. What is the prettiest flower? What juice tastes best? The answers to these questions are opinions. You might think apple juice tastes best. Another student might think orange juice tastes best. Collecting observations would not help a scientist decide which of you is right. Science cannot answer questions about tastes or personal opinions.

Lightning Lab

Questions and Answers

Think about something you would like to investigate. List the questions you would ask. Talk with a partner. How would your questions help you look for answers?

2. **Underline** the question below that science cannot answer.

   Do plants need water to grow?

   Is baseball a better sport than basketball?

3. **Generate** What other question might the boy in the picture ask?

   ....

   ....

   ....

Which soil works best?

How much water do these plants need?

myscienceonline.com | Got it? | 60-Second Video

Alone or in Teams

Sometimes scientists work alone, but sometimes scientists can learn more by working together. When scientists work together they can share information and discoveries. Scientists who are investigating how to keep insects from eating crops might each try different methods and then compare their results. Scientists might take turns caring for their crops.

These students use hand lenses to observe.

4. **Describe** What is another way scientists might work together?

....

....

Got it? ⬤ 3.NS.1, 3.NS.2, 3.NS.3

5. **Draw Conclusions** If you were acting like a scientist in class, what would you be doing? Write three things.

....

....

6. **UNLOCK THE BIG ?** A student asks the question, "What is the best color for a bike?" Can science answer this question? Explain.

....

....

⬛ **Stop!** I need help with ....

⏸ **Wait!** I have a question about ....

▶ **Go!** Now I know ....

Lesson 2

What skills do scientists use?

Envision It!

3.NS.7 Keep accurate records in a notebook during investigations and communicate findings to others using graphs, charts, maps and models through oral and written reports.

Look at the time-elapsed photo of a hurricane.
Tell what you can observe about hurricanes.

Inquiry **Explore It!**

How can observations help you make an inference?

☑ **1.** Place the clear blue sheet over the color wheel. **Observe.**

☑ **2.** Repeat Step 1 with the clear red sheet and then the clear yellow sheet.

☑ **3.** Discuss the changes you **observed.**

Materials

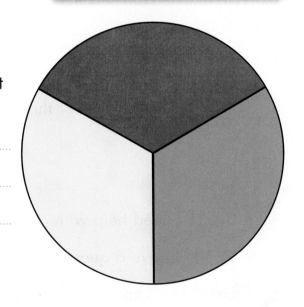

red sheet

blue sheet

yellow sheet

Explain Your Results

4. Infer How are blue, red, and yellow different from purple, orange, and green?

....

....

....

5. Think about the skills you used. Tell how your **observations** helped you make your **inference.**

myscienceonline.com | **Explore It!** Animation

3.NS.8 Identify simple patterns in data and propose explanations to account for the patterns. (Also **3.NS.3**)

UNLOCK
THE BIG

I will know how to use process skills such as observation, prediction, and measurement.

Word to Know

infer

Science Skills

Scientists use process skills to learn about objects, places, or events. Observation is a process skill. When you use your five senses to find out about something, you observe. Your senses include sight, hearing, touch, taste, and smell.

Scientists often use tools to make observations. A satellite is a tool that helps scientists observe Earth's weather. Data from satellites are often displayed on weather maps. The weather map below shows hurricanes, which are strong storms.

1. **Observe** Look at the picture below. What is one observation you can make?

....

....

....

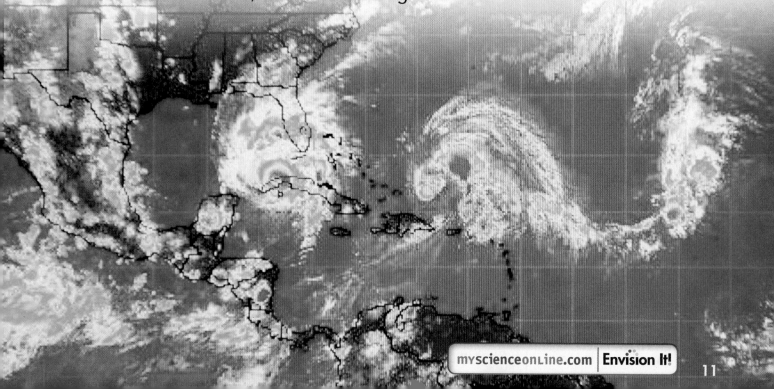

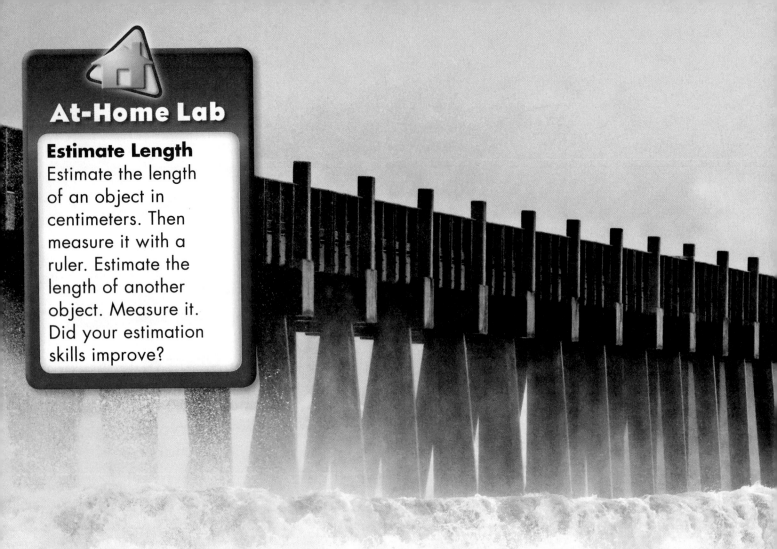

Estimate and Measure

Scientists sometimes estimate when they make observations. To estimate means to make a careful guess. A scientist standing on the pier in the picture might feel the wind pushing hard against his body. He might estimate that the wind is blowing about 70 or 80 kilometers per hour.

To find the exact wind speed, the scientist would make a measurement. A measurement is a number that tells how much or how many. Scientists often use tools to measure. An anemometer is a tool that can measure the speed of the wind.

2. **CHALLENGE** Suppose the pier in the picture is 20 feet high. Explain how you could use this information to estimate the height of the waves.

....

....

....

....

 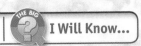

anemometer

Infer and Predict

Some data and observations are facts. For example, the statement "The wave crashed into the pier" is a fact. You can use facts to **infer,** or draw a conclusion. Scientists infer what they think is happening based on what they observe or based on prior knowledge. For example, a scientist observing the waves in the picture might infer that a hurricane is coming on shore.

Observations also can help you to predict. When you predict, you tell what you think will happen in the future. For example, a scientist might predict that the waves will get bigger as the hurricane gets closer to shore.

3. Predict What is another prediction you could make based on your observations of this picture?

....

....

....

....

Classify

Classify means to sort objects, events, or living things based on their properties. When you classify, you put similar things into groups or categories. Scientists use the Saffir-Simpson Hurricane Scale to classify and compare hurricanes. The scale groups hurricanes into categories according to wind speed.

Saffir-Simpson Hurricane Scale		
Category	**Wind Speed**	
	miles per hour	**kilometers per hour**
5	more than 155	more than 249
4	131–155	210–249
3	111–130	178–209
2	96–110	154–177
1	74–95	119–153

1. **Classify** A hurricane has a wind speed of 158 kilometers per hour. What is the hurricane's category?

2. **Compare** Hurricane A has a wind speed of 137 kilometers per hour. Hurricane B has a wind speed of 135 miles per hour. Are the two hurricanes in the same category? Explain.

3. **Analyze** The graph below shows wind speeds for Hurricane C in miles per hour (mph). How did the hurricane change on Day 4? Use the word *category* in your answer.

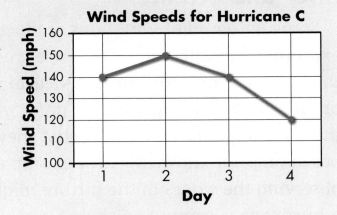

Wind Speeds for Hurricane C

myscienceonline.com | Got it? 60-Second Video

Interpret and Explain Data

Scientists work together to interpret their data and form scientific explanations. A good explanation uses observations, inferences, prior knowledge, measurements, and data from an investigation. Scientists use all this information to explain how things happen naturally.

For example, scientists are trying to develop the ability to forecast when hurricanes will form. They use observations, weather data, and their knowledge of past storms to predict where hurricanes will strike and how strong they will be. This information can help people stay safe.

4. Underline five things that a good explanation uses.

HURRICANE CENTER
PREDICTION CENTER
RNATIONAL UNIVERSITY

Got it? 🕐 3.NS.7

5. **Apply** Name a process skill. How can it help scientists learn about hurricanes?

....

....

6. **Predict** What might happen if a person building a house estimated but did not measure the length of a piece of wood?

....

....

⬛ **Stop!** I need help with ....

⏸ **Wait!** I have a question about ....

▶ **Go!** Now I know ....

How do scientists answer questions?

3.NS.5 Use measurement skills and apply appropriate units when collecting data. 3.NS.6 Test predictions with multiple trials. (Also 3.NS.2)

Tell how you think this model can help scientists answer questions.

Inquiry Explore It!

How can a model help answer questions?

☐ **1.** Spread out your fingers and put your hand flat on a piece of paper. **Measure** the length of the longest finger. Measure its height. **Record.**

☐ **2. Make a model** by tracing your hand. Measure the length of the longest finger on your model. Measure its height. Record.

Explain Your Results

3. Scientists use models to help them answer questions, but models have limitations. Does your **model** account for all your **observations** of your real finger? Explain.

....

....

....

....

Materials

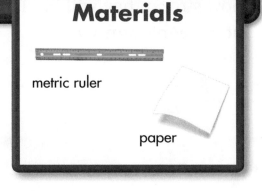

metric ruler

paper

Measurements

	Length (mm)	Height (mm)
Finger		
Model of a finger		

myscienceonline.com | **Explore It!** Animation

3.DP.9 Present evidence using mathematical representations (graphs, data tables). (Also **3.NS.8, 3.4.1**)

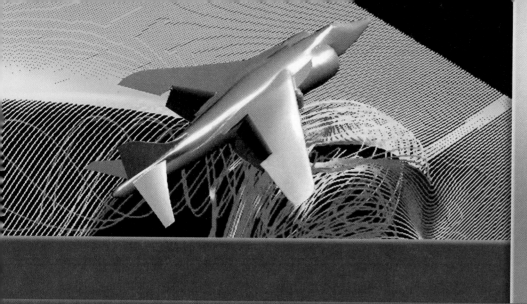

UNLOCK THE BIG ?

I will know how scientists use experiments and other types of investigations to answer questions.

Word to Know

model

Kinds of Investigations

Scientists are like detectives. They investigate, or look for answers, using organized steps. Different questions require different kinds of investigations. Some investigations involve observing and describing things or events. Other investigations may involve collecting samples or building models. An investigation can be any organized way of looking for answers.

An experiment is an investigation carried out under carefully controlled conditions. A scientist might do an experiment to find out if a new medicine works better than an old medicine.

1. ◉ **Text Features** What does the heading tell about this page?

....

....

....

2. **Analyze** These students are observing and describing flowers. Write what question you think they are investigating.

....

....

....

....

Scientific Methods

Suppose you want to classify animals by how they keep warm. You might do an experiment to test fur's ability to keep heat in water. When scientists do an experiment, they use scientific methods. Scientific methods include the steps shown below.

3. Hypothesize Write another hypothesis for the question.

....

....

....

....

....

....

4. [CHALLENGE] How do you know your answer to question 3 is a good hypothesis?

....

....

....

Ask a question.
You might have a question about something you observe.

What material is best for keeping heat in water?

State your hypothesis.
A hypothesis is a possible answer to your question. Hypotheses can be tested.

If I wrap the jar in fake fur, then the water will stay warm the longest because fake fur will keep heat in.

Identify and control variables.
Variables are things in an experiment that can change. For a fair test, you choose just one variable to change. Keep all other variables the same.

Test other materials. Put the same amount of warm water in other jars that are the same size and shape.

Test your hypothesis.

Make a plan to test your hypothesis. Include multiple trials by doing your test many times. That way, if one measurement is off, the data you collect will still be useful. Gather materials and tools. Then follow your plan.

Collect and record your data.

Keep records of what you do and find. Records can be notes, pictures, charts, or graphs.

Interpret your data.

Organize your notes and records.

State your conclusion.

Your conclusion is a decision you make based on your data. Communicate what you found. Tell whether or not your data supported your hypothesis.

Fake fur kept the water warm longest because fake fur kept the heat in. My data supported my hypothesis.

Go further.

Use what you learn from your experiment to do more experiments. Think of new questions to test.

5. ◎ **Compare and Contrast** What is the same about all three jars?

....

....

What is different?

....

....

6. **Identify** (Circle) the tool that is used in this experiment.

7. **Apply** Use the results of this experiment to ask another question that could be tested.

....

....

....

....

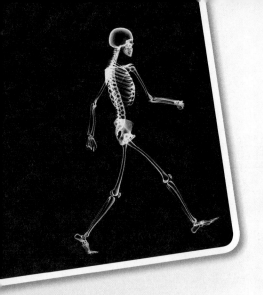

This computer model shows how the skeleton moves as the human body walks.

8. Infer How do you think this model of the human body can help scientists?

....

....

....

....

9. Explain How can this model help you understand the real solar system?

....

....

....

....

Models

Another way scientists investigate is with models. A **model** is a copy of something. Models help scientists understand how things work. Models also help scientists study things that are very small, large, or difficult to understand.

Some models are built out of materials such as paper and plastic. Other models are made using a program on a computer. For example, scientists have used computers to build models of the human body. These computer models help scientists better understand how different parts of the body, such as the heart and the skeletal system, work. The models can also be used to train doctors.

Models are useful, but they are not the same as the real thing. For example, a computer model might show how a person's body fits together. But it might not show how well the body will function.

This model is a copy of the solar system, a large group of objects in space.

Surveys

Scientists also use surveys to investigate. A survey is a list of questions or choices. Scientists can give the list to many people and learn from their answers. For example, scientists give surveys to patients to learn about their symptoms. Then scientists can interpret the data and draw inferences. The surveys and data can help scientists make new medicines.

10. Infer How are surveys a type of investigation?

....

....

Go Green

Recycling Survey
Write a survey to find out what materials people recycle in their homes. Ask about materials such as paper, plastic, glass, and metal cans. Ask your survey questions to ten people. Record the results. Do you see a pattern in the data?

Got it?

🔘 3.NS.2, 3.NS.5, 3.NS.6

11. Summarize Name three ways scientists investigate.

....

....

12. Investigate Grass does not grow well under a tree. Write a hypothesis that explains why this might be true. How can you test your hypothesis?

....

....

....

⏹ **Stop!** I need help with ....

⏸ **Wait!** I have a question about ....

▶ **Go!** Now I know ....

Lesson 4

How do scientists communicate?

Envision It!

3.NS.7 Keep accurate records in a notebook during investigations and communicate findings to others using graphs, charts, maps and models through oral and written reports. 3.NS.9 Compare the results of an investigation with the prediction. (Also 3.NS.5, 3.NS.8)

Tell how keeping records can help these scientists share information.

Inquiry **Explore It!**

How can scientists communicate what they learn?

☐ **1.** Conduct a survey. Think of a question you want to ask, such as "What is your favorite color?"

☐ **2.** Write your question in the chart.

☐ **3.** **Record** your data. Use tally marks.

☐ **4.** **Communicate** Make a bar graph using your data. Share this with your class.

Explain Your Results

5. How did your bar graph help you **communicate** what you learned?

....

....

....

....

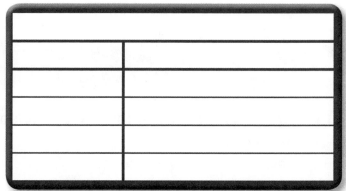

Bar Graph

myscienceonline.com | **Explore It!** Animation

3.DP.9 Present evidence using mathematical representations (graphs, data tables). (Also **3.NS.3**)

I will know how to describe a procedure and record data. I will know how scientists communicate.

Words to Know

procedure   bar graph
chart

Communication

Communication is an important part of science investigations. Scientists communicate with each other to share what they learn. They also question and check each other's work. When scientists share information in this way, their explanations are more thorough and better informed.

One way scientists check each other's work is to replicate, or repeat, an experiment. A good experiment can be repeated. For this reason, scientists must keep careful records of their experiments. Other scientists can repeat the same procedure if they know exactly how it was done.

1. **Infer** The scientists in the picture are investigating algae, a group of living things usually found in water. What kind of records do you think the scientists are keeping?

....

....

....

....

2. Identify Look at the procedure. (Circle) the units that were used to make measurements.

3. Analyze The person who wrote this procedure knew that warm water loses heat over time. What was the person trying to find out?

....

....

....

4. Describe What words could be added to help describe the procedure?

....

....

....

Plan an Experiment

When you plan an experiment, you write a procedure. A **procedure** is a plan for testing a hypothesis. It describes the materials you will use and the steps you will follow. Write the procedure clearly so someone else can follow your steps and get the same results. Tell what units you will use in your measurements.

As you plan an experiment, think carefully about the question you are trying to answer. Figure out what you know and what you want to find out.

A procedure describes exactly how an experiment is done.

Question: What material is best for keeping heat in water?

Hypothesis: If I wrap a jar in fake fur, then it will keep the water warm the longest.

Materials: 1 jar covered in fake fur, 1 jar covered in brown paper, 1 jar covered in blue paper, warm water, 3 thermometers, plastic wrap, 3 rubber bands, clock

Procedure:
1. Label the jars A, B, and C.
2. Add a thermometer to each jar.
3. Fill each jar with the same amount of warm water.
4. Quickly cover the jars with plastic wrap and rubber bands.
5. Measure the starting temperature in degrees Celsius.
6. Measure and record how many minutes it takes for the temperature to change in each jar.
7. Empty the jars. Repeat steps 2 through 6.

THE BIG ? I Will Know...

Keep Records

When scientists investigate, they do the same experiment several times. Each time is called a trial. Scientists keep careful records of their results for each trial.

You can keep records in many ways. You can use numbers or words. Sometimes an easy way to record what happens is to draw a picture or a map. A chart is a way to organize what you record. A **chart** is a kind of list. You can also use a graph to organize data. A **bar graph** is a graph that helps you compare data and see patterns.

6. **Explain** Why are there two rows for each type of material in the chart below?

....

....

....

7. **Express Data** Use your science notebook to draw pictures and write about the experiment.

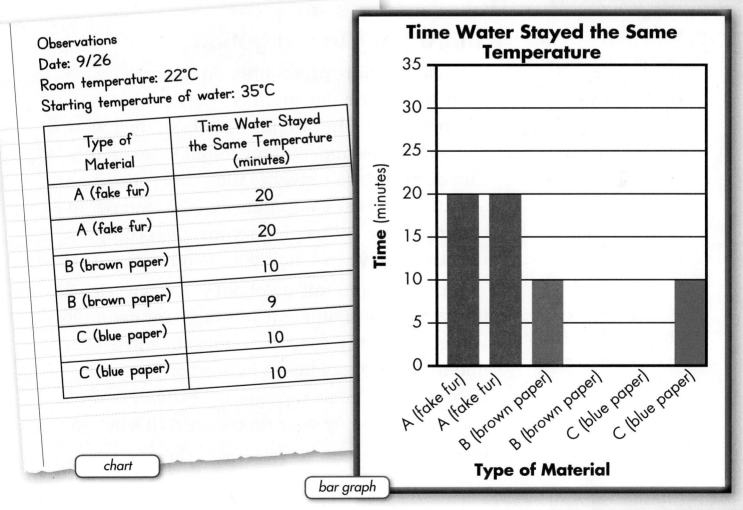

Observations
Date: 9/26
Room temperature: 22°C
Starting temperature of water: 35°C

Type of Material	Time Water Stayed the Same Temperature (minutes)
A (fake fur)	20
A (fake fur)	20
B (brown paper)	10
B (brown paper)	9
C (blue paper)	10
C (blue paper)	10

chart

Time Water Stayed the Same Temperature

Time (minutes)

Type of Material

bar graph

5. **Communicate Data** Complete the missing bars in the bar graph above.

25

8. Interpret The boy in the picture is communicating. What might he be telling his classmates?

9. Recall Why is it important for scientists to communicate with each other?

Share Your Investigation

Scientists share procedures, data, and conclusions with one another. They do this in different ways. They might talk about their work at a scientific meeting. Or they might write an article that describes their investigation and conclusions. Scientists also use computers and the Internet to communicate. By keeping records on a computer, they can easily send their data to other scientists.

You can communicate about your own science investigations in different ways too. For example, you might write a report or a journal entry. You might give a presentation in front of your class. Or you might create a poster, an exhibit, or a portfolio to display your procedure and what you have learned.

myscienceonLine.com | **Got it?** 60-Second Video

Repeat an Investigation

Scientists check each other's work. One scientist will repeat another scientist's experiment so they can compare evidence and explanations. An explanation is only considered true if another person can follow the procedure and get similar results.

If two scientists follow the same procedure and get different results, they can discuss why. They can use this information to make the procedure better for the next scientist.

Lightning Lab

Construct a Chart
Go outside. Look at plants you see. Classify the plants in two ways. Make a chart to record your data. Discuss your chart with a partner.

10. Analyze Why would scientists want other scientists to repeat their experiment?

....

....

Got it? 3.NS.5, 3.NS.7, 3.NS.8, 3.NS.9

11. Summarize Name four ways scientists keep records.

....

12. Describe What information should a procedure include?

....

....

....

⬛ **Stop!** I need help with ....

⏸ **Wait!** I have a question about ....

▶ **Go!** Now I know ....

How do scientists use tools and stay safe?

3.4.1 Choose and use the appropriate tools to estimate and measure length, mass and temperature in SI units. **3.NS.4** Perform investigations using appropriate tools and technology that will extend the senses. (Also **3.NS.5**)

Envision It!

Tell how you think microscopes help you view small objects, such as insects.

Inquiry Explore It!

How can a tool help scientists observe?

☐ **1.** Find how much water is in a cup. First, **measure** 50 mL of water from the cup into a graduated cylinder. **Record** the measurement.

Then, empty the graduated cylinder into the second cup.
Repeat until you have measured all the water from the first cup.

☐ **2.** Calculate the total amount that was in the first cup at the start.

Explain Your Results

3. Compare your total with the amount other groups **measured.** Are the totals the same? Discuss.

4. How did the graduated cylinder help you make your comparisons?

....

....

Materials

funnel

graduated cylinder

plastic cup

plastic cup with water

Volume in Cup (mL)	
Measurement	**Volume (mL)**
1st	
2nd	
3rd	
Total	

myscienceonline.com | **Explore It!** Animation

3.NS.5 Use measurement skills and apply appropriate units when collecting data. (Also **3.NS.7, 3.4.1, 3.DP.9**)

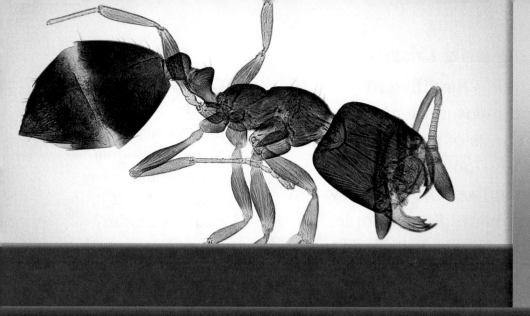

Science Tools

Scientists use many different kinds of tools. A **tool** is an object used to do work. You can use tools to observe. Tools can help you measure volume, temperature, length, distance, and mass. Tools can help you collect and record data. Data are facts and information that you observe. You can record data on a computer. Computers can also help you share observations with others and find new information. Taking pictures with a camera is another way of using a tool to record data.

Some tools you use to observe make objects appear larger. Binoculars are a tool that helps you see things that are far away. For example, binoculars help you see birds nesting in trees.

1. **Underline** four things you can do with tools.

2. **Apply** How might you use binoculars like these?

....

....

....

....

Tools for Measuring and Observing

Scientists use different tools for different kinds of observations and measurements. Most measurement tools have units of measure. A **unit of measure** is the quantity you use to measure something. Scientists use units of the metric system when they make measurements. For example, meters and centimeters are metric units used to measure length. You might be familiar with units of the United States system. In that system, feet and inches are used to measure length.

3. Compare
(Circle) the thermometer that shows the higher temperature. How much higher is it, in degrees Celsius?

....

....

Thermometers measure temperature. Thermometers are marked in degrees Celsius (°C) and degrees Fahrenheit (°F). Scientists usually record data in degrees Celsius.

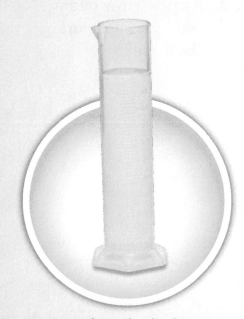

A graduated cylinder can be used to measure volume, or the amount of space an object takes up. Volume is measured in milliliters (mL).

Clocks and stopwatches are used to measure time.

Scientists use rulers and metersticks to measure length and distance in meters (m) and centimeters (cm).

4. Compare Look at the balance. How do the masses compare?

A balance like the one above can be used to measure an object's mass in grams.

Lightning Lab

Which Tool Is It?
Describe one of the tools in this lesson to a partner. Do not say what it is. Have your partner guess the tool. Then switch roles. Guess a tool your partner describes.

5. Apply Which tool would you use to study the parts of an ant?

6. Apply Use a hand lens. Observe a tool on one of these two pages. What did you observe?

Microscopes use several lenses to make objects appear larger. Microscopes let you see more detail.

A hand lens enlarges objects too. It does not enlarge objects as much as a microscope does. It is easier to carry, though.

Safety

You need to be careful when using tools or doing other scientific activities. Some tools, such as safety goggles, help protect you. Below is a list of safety rules to remember.

- Listen to your teacher's instructions.

- Read each activity carefully.

- Never taste or smell materials unless your teacher tells you to.

- Wear safety goggles, wear gloves, and tie hair back when needed.

- Handle scissors and other equipment carefully.

- Keep your workplace neat and clean.

- Clean up spills immediately.

- Tell your teacher immediately about accidents or if you see something that looks unsafe.

- Wash your hands well after every activity.

- Return all materials to their proper places.

7. **Explain** Why is it important to wash your hands?

....

....

....

8. **Elaborate** Write a new safety tip to add to the list.

....

....

....

....

....

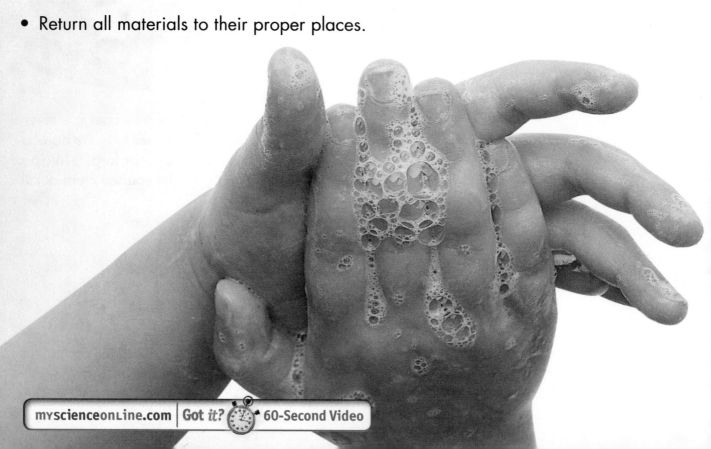

myscienceonline.com | Got it? | 60-Second Video

Investigating Safely

When scientists explore underwater, they need certain tools to stay safe. The scuba divers need tanks filled with oxygen to breathe and wet suits to protect their skin.

9. **Suggest** What equipment do you use to stay safe when you play outside?

....

....

....

Got it?   🔵 3.4.1, 3.NS.4, 3.NS.5

10. **Infer** Why do you think it is important to tell your teacher about accidents immediately?

....

....

11. **Explain** Choose one tool from this lesson and explain why it is important to scientists.

....

....

⬛ **Stop!** I need help with ....

⏸ **Wait!** I have a question about ....

▶ **Go!** Now I know ....

How does a microscope make your observations easier?

microscope

hand lens

yarn

color newspaper

Follow a Procedure

☐ **1. Observe** a piece of yarn and a photo from a color newspaper.
Record your observations.

☐ **2.** Observe the yarn and the photo with a hand lens.
Record your observations.

Inquiry Skill Scientists use tools to make **observations.**

Be careful! **Handle microscopes with care.**

Observations

Item	No Tool	Hand Lens	Microscope
Yarn			
Photo			

3.NS.4 Perform investigations using appropriate tools and technology that will extend the senses. (Also **3.NS.3**)

☐ **3.** Observe using a microscope. First, place the yarn on the stage of the microscope. Then, look through the eyepiece. Record your observations.

☐ **4.** Repeat Step 3 with the photo.

Analyze and Conclude

5. Communicate   How were your **observations** different when you used different tools?

....

....

6. Draw a Conclusion   How does a microscope help make observation easier?

....

....

7. Infer   When might a hand lens be more useful than a microscope?

....

....

....

8. **UNLOCK** **THE BIG** **?** **Investigate**   List two other objects a scientist could observe better using a microscope.

....

....

3.NS.3, 3.NS.7

Observe Insect Behavior

You can practice observing by watching insects. Go outside with an adult and look at insects on tree trunks, on leaves, under rocks, or in cracks along sidewalks. Do not touch any insect. Bring a notebook to draw an insect. Observe it for several minutes. To keep records, write down observations about how it acts. Compare observations with the adult who is with you.

Illustrate Draw the insect.

Observe Record what you observe about how the insect acts.

....

....

Infer Use the evidence you observed to make an inference. What do you think the insect was doing?

....

Vocabulary Smart Cards

scientist
investigate
inquiry
infer
model
procedure
chart
bar graph
tool
unit of measure

Play a Game!

Cut out the Vocabulary Smart Cards.

Cover the words on the front of each card with sticky notes.

Use the list of words above to guess which word goes with each picture. Write the word on the sticky note.

Then remove the sticky note to see if you were correct.

infer

inferir

scientist

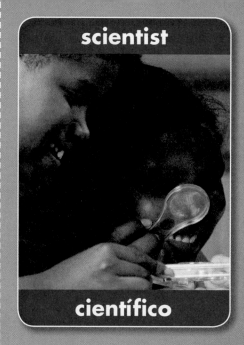

científico

model

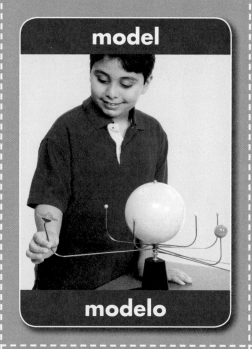

modelo

investigate

investigar

procedure

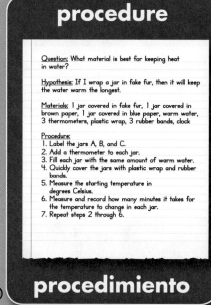

Question: What material is best for keeping heat in water?

Hypothesis: If I wrap a jar in fake fur, then it will keep the water warm the longest.

Materials: 1 jar covered in fake fur, 1 jar covered in brown paper, 1 jar covered in blue paper, warm water, 3 thermometers, plastic wrap, 3 rubber bands, clock

Procedure:
1. Label the jars A, B, and C.
2. Add a thermometer to each jar.
3. Fill each jar with the same amount of warm water.
4. Quickly cover the jars with plastic wrap and rubber bands.
5. Measure the starting temperature in degrees Celsius.
6. Measure and record how many minutes it takes for the temperature to change in each jar.
7. Repeat steps 2 through 6.

procedimiento

inquiry

investigación

person who asks questions about the natural world

Write a sentence using this word.

....

....

....

persona cuyo trabajo implica hacer preguntas sobre el mundo y la naturaleza

to draw a conclusion

Write the noun form of this word.

....

....

....

....

sacar una conclusión

Interactive Vocabulary

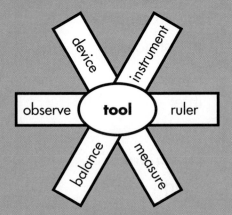

Make a Word Wheel!

Choose a vocabulary word and write it in the center of the Word Wheel graphic organizer. Write synonyms or related words on the wheel spokes.

to look for answers

Write the noun form of this word.

....

....

....

....

buscar respuestas

a copy of something

Draw an example.

copia de algo

the process of asking questions

Write a sentence using the verb form of this word.

....

....

....

....

proceso de hacer preguntas

a plan for testing a hypothesis

Use a dictionary. Write the verb form of the word.

....

....

....

plan que se usa para poner a prueba una hipótesis

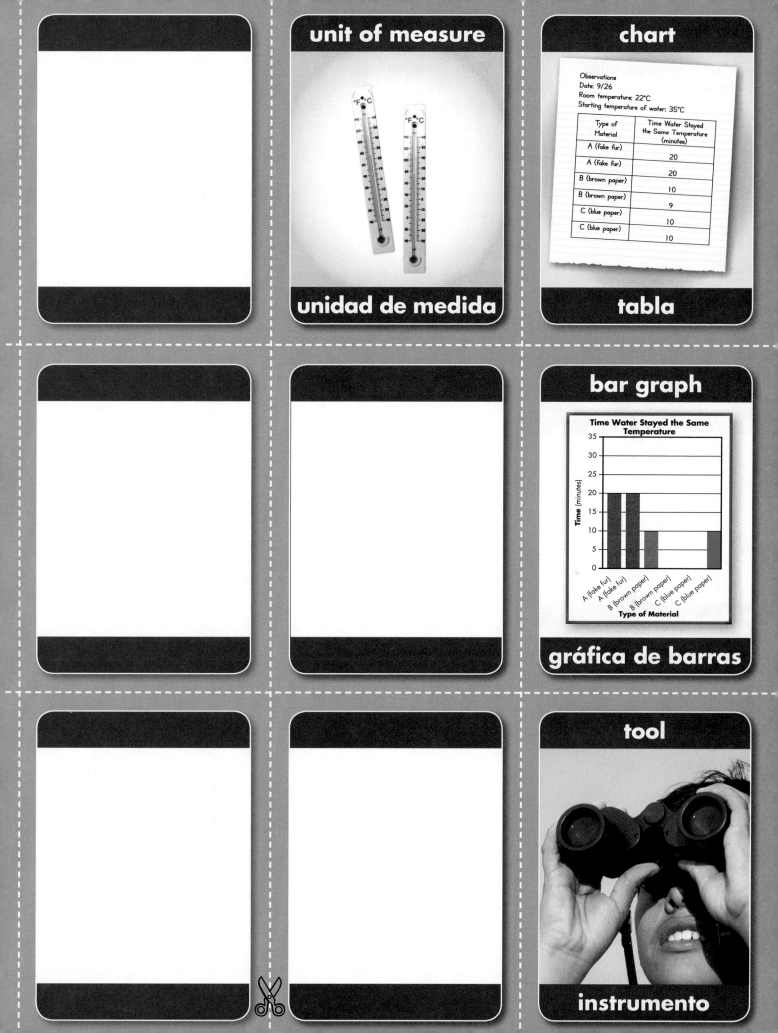

a kind of list

Write a sentence using this word.

....

....

....

....

tipo de lista

---

quantity you use to measure

Write three examples.

....

....

....

....

cantidad que se usa para medir

---

a graph that helps you compare data and see patterns

Draw an example.

gráfica que ayuda a comparar datos y ver patrones

---

object used to do work

Write three examples.

....

....

....

....

objeto que se usa para trabajar

Lesson 1

What questions do scientists ask?

- Scientists ask questions about the natural world.
- Scientists ask questions that can be answered through investigations.

Lesson 2

What skills do scientists use?

- Scientists observe by using their five senses.
- Scientists infer and predict based on observations.
- Scientists use their results to form explanations.

Lesson 3

How do scientists answer questions?

- Scientists answer questions using experiments and other kinds of investigations.
- Scientific methods are organized steps for investigations.

Lesson 4

How do scientists communicate?

- Scientists communicate to share what they learn.
- When scientists investigate, they write a procedure.
- Good records include words, charts, and graphs.

Lesson 5

How do scientists use tools and stay safe?

- Scientists use tools to observe, to measure, and to collect and record data.
- Safety is important when doing science.

Chapter Review

REVIEW THE BIG ? What is science?

Lesson 1 🕐 3.NS.1, 3.NS.2, 3.NS.3

What questions do scientists ask?

1. **Vocabulary** Someone who asks questions about the natural world is a(n) _____.
   A. engineer
   B. model
   C. scientist
   D. teacher

2. **Apply** What is a question that cannot be answered through an investigation?

_____

_____

Lesson 2 🕐 3.NS.7

What skills do scientists use?

3. **Observe** What five senses do scientists use when they make observations?

_____

_____

4. **Name** List three things a good investigation needs.

_____

_____

_____

Lesson 3 🕐 3.NS.2, 3.NS.5, 3.NS.6

How do scientists answer questions?

5. **Write About It** Suggest two ways a model could help you better understand the solar system.

_____

_____

_____

_____

_____

6. **List** What are three steps that a good experiment should include?

_____

_____

_____

7. **Conclude** You measure your heart rate at 70 beats per minute after resting and 100 beats per minute after exercising. Over several days you take more measurements and get similar results. What can you conclude?

_____

_____

Lesson 4   3.NS.5, 3.NS.7, 3.NS.8, 3.NS.9

How do scientists communicate?

8. **Text Features** How do graphs help you communicate the results of an experiment?

Lesson 5   3.4.1, 3.NS.4, 3.NS.5

How do scientists use tools and stay safe?

9. Determine Name this tool. Tell how you could use it.

10. APPLY THE BIG **?**   **What is science?**

Think about scientists. How do they work? Use the vocabulary words *tool*, *investigate*, and *model* in your explanation.

Multiple Choice

1 Which could you measure with the tool shown in this picture?

A. the mass of a rock

B. the length of a pencil

C. the temperature of the air

D. the volume of a liquid

 3.NS.4

Constructed Response

2 It is important for scientists to keep accurate records during an investigation. Describe three ways scientists can communicate their findings.

....

....

....

....

 3.NS.7

Extended Response

3 Trey wanted to test three different brands of paper towels to see which one held the most water. He added water 1 ounce at a time to each paper towel. Once the paper towel was completely wet, he recorded his results. The bar graph below shows his results.

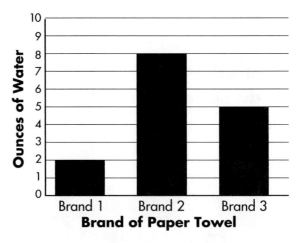

Why do you think Brand 2 held the most water?

....

....

After seeing these results, why do you think people would buy Brand 2?

....

....

3.NS.8

Biography

Cary Fowler

Cary Fowler helped run the Global Seed Vault project.

Cary Fowler was born in Tennessee and spent his summers on a farm. Later he became a plant scientist. Fowler became worried about the plants we use as crops. Through history, people have used more than 10,000 different types of plants for food. Now there are only 150 types left. Fowler asked, "What if we lose even more?" Diseases, natural disasters, and war can all wipe out plants.

Fowler moved to Italy to help run a project called the Global Seed Vault. The Global Seed Vault is a tool used by plant scientists. It is a giant freezer buried in the ground near the North Pole in Norway. The vault is used to save different types of plant seeds from all over the world. The vault is big enough to hold more than 2 billion seeds.

The goal of the vault is to save seeds for thousands of years. Then, even if we lose a type of plant, we can use the seeds to plant more!

APPLY THE BIG ?

What did Cary Fowler infer about the crops we have left?

....

....

Where can this tiny robot fly?

Technology and the Design Process

Try It! How can you design a parachute?

Lesson 1 What is technology?
3.4.2, 3.NS.4

Lesson 2 What is a machine?
3.4.2, 3.NS.4

Lesson 3 What is the design process?
3.DP.1, 3.DP.3 3.DP.4, 3.DP.7, 3.DP.11

Investigate It! What makes a bridge strong?

This is an image of a piece of technology that is still being developed. Some scientists think that in the future, the robotic fly will be able to locate people who are trapped in a collapsed building. It can fit in tiny places where a person may not fit.

Predict Why do you think the robot was designed to look like a fly?

....

....

How can technology affect our lives?

How can you design a parachute?

☐ **1. Design** a parachute that will slow the fall of a metal washer dropped from a height of 2 meters.

☐ **2. Communicate** Draw and label your design.

string plastic bag

paper aluminum foil

metal washer

scissors timer or stopwatch

metric ruler

masking tape

☐ **3.** Build your parachute. Ask your teacher to test it 3 times. **Record.** Compare your results with others.

Inquiry Skill
You **communicate** when you draw and label diagrams.

Parachute	Trial 1 (s)	Trial 2 (s)	Trial 3 (s)
1			
2			

☐ **4.** Evaluate your design. Improve it. Repeat Step 3.

Explain Your Results

5. UNLOCK THE BIG **? Communicate** Which parachute dropped most slowly?

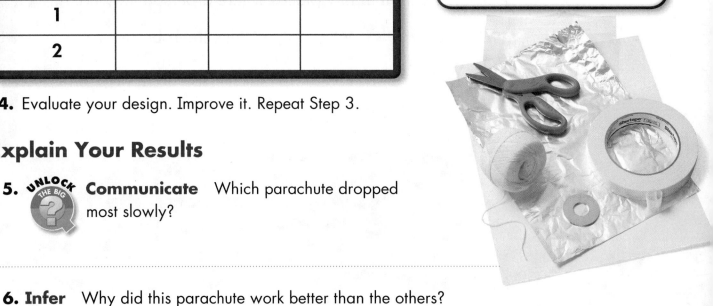

....

6. Infer Why did this parachute work better than the others?

....

....

3.DP.1 Identify a need or problem to be solved. **3.DP.8** Evaluate and test the design using measurement. **3.DP.10** Communicate the solution including evidence using mathematical representations (graphs, data tables), drawings or prototypes. **3.DP.11** Communicate how to improve the solution. (Also **3.DP.5, 3.DP.7**)

Main Idea and Details

- The **main idea** is the most important idea in a reading selection.
- Supporting **details** tell more about the main idea.

Recycled Energy

Technology has changed the way we get energy. A water-powered mill uses technology to get energy from the flowing water of a river. A solar panel can be placed on the roof of a house. It gathers energy from the sun. Energy from the wind can be captured by wind turbines. This energy helps to produce electricity. Technology allows us to recycle energy, which helps protect the environment.

Practice it!

Complete the graphic organizer below. Use it to help you list the main idea and details from the paragraph you read above.

wind turbine

Main Idea

Detail   **Detail**   **Detail**

What is technology?

3.4.2 Define the uses and types of simple machines and utilize simple machines in the solution to a real world problem. **3.NS.4** Perform investigations using appropriate tools and technology that will extend the senses.

Envision It!

What do you think the technology in the picture is? How do you think it works?

my planet Diary

DISCOVERY

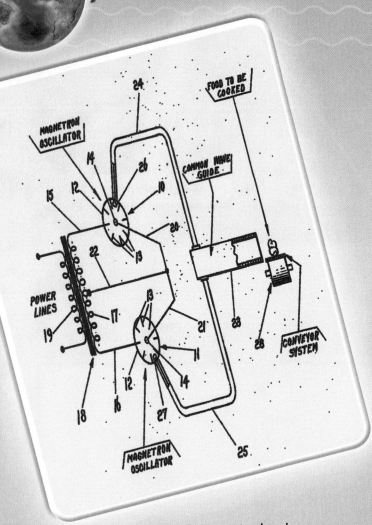

Percy Spencer's sketch helped him build the first microwave oven.

Sometimes technology becomes useful in unplanned ways. In 1946, Percy Spencer was working to improve radar. He was performing tests using microwave energy.

One day Spencer stood near the microwave energy. He noticed that a candy bar in his pocket melted. Curious, he put popcorn kernels near the microwave energy. They rapidly popped into fluffy pieces.

Spencer found that the microwave could quickly cook foods. He made a drawing that led to the first microwave oven.

Infer Why was it important for Percy Spencer to keep asking questions after his candy bar melted?

....

....

....

UNLOCK THE BIG ?

I will know how technology solves problems and provides solutions.

Word to Know

technology

Problems and Solutions

Science helps people understand the way the world works. Technology helps people solve problems and improve their lives. **Technology** is the use of science knowledge to invent tools and new ways of doing things.

Discoveries in science are helping people solve some big problems. For example, people use energy for many things. They use energy to cook food and heat their homes. But we may be running out of some energy sources. The discovery of how to use solar energy may help solve this problem. Solar energy is energy that comes directly from the sun's rays. Solar panels gather the sun's rays. Next, they change this energy into electricity.

Solar panels provide a new way of getting energy.

1. **Underline** the definition of technology.

2. CHALLENGE Solar panels work well in some places but not others. Explain why this is true.

....

....

Signals from satellites can track the exact location of a car.

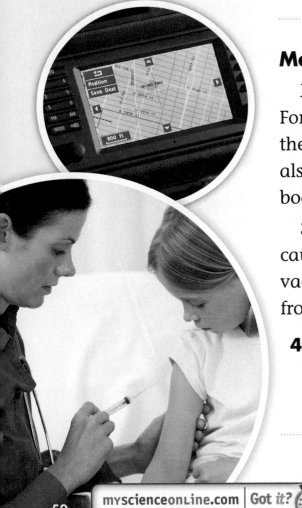

Scientific Discoveries and Technology

Scientific discoveries usually are made by scientists. Engineers use this knowledge to develop technologies that change and improve the way people live. Here are some examples.

Transportation

People on ships once had to figure out where they were by looking at stars. Now sailors can use Global Positioning System (GPS) technology. This technology relies on space satellites that send signals to Earth. Each ship's GPS computer uses the signals to figure out the ship's location.

3. **Explain** How has GPS technology made transportation easier?

....

....

Medicine

X rays were discovered more than 100 years ago. For the first time, doctors could look inside the body without touching it. Today, doctors also use digital technology to look inside people's bodies.

Scientists discovered that viruses and bacteria cause disease. This led to the development of vaccines. Vaccines are medicines that protect you from disease. Vaccines are a type of technology.

4. **Interpret** This child is receiving a vaccine, a type of technology. What is another technology that you see in this photograph?

....

Computer Technology

A computer stores information. Computers also process and send information with great speed. Computer technology is everywhere. A digital watch tells time with a computer chip. Calculators, cameras, appliances, and cars all use these chips.

Computer chips are being made smaller and smaller. Music players, game players, and phones can process as much information as whole desktop computers once could.

Computer chips can send and receive huge numbers of electronic data signals very quickly.

5. **Predict** How would your life be different if computer technology did not exist?

....

....

Got it?   🔘 3.4.2, 3.NS.4

6. **Give Examples** Name two technologies. Tell how they have changed people's lives.

....

....

7. ◎ **Draw Conclusions** How can one technology lead to the development of other technologies?

....

....

■ **Stop!** I need help with ....

❚❚ **Wait!** I have a question about ....

▶ **Go!** Now I know ....

What is a machine?

3.4.2 Define the uses and types of simple machines and utilize simple machines in the solution to a real world problem.
3.NS.4 Perform investigations using appropriate tools and technology that will extend the senses.

Envision It!

Tell how the pole helps this vaulter jump higher.

Inquiry Explore It!

How can a simple machine solve a problem?

Pat and Chris want to know whose cup of marbles is heavier. All they have is a ruler and a pencil.

☐ **1. Make a Model   Design** a way to solve this problem. Use a simple machine.

☐ **2. Communicate**   Draw your solution.

☐ **3.** Test your design. Which cup is heavier?

Materials

2 cups of metal marbles

unsharpened pencil

ruler

Explain Your Results

4. Name the simple machine you used.

5. Draw a Conclusion   What is another way you could use your simple machine?

myscienceonLine.com | **Explore It!** Animation

3.DP.3 Document the design throughout the entire design process. **3.DP.4** Select a solution to the need or problem. **3.DP.6** Create the solution through a prototype. (Also **3.DP.2**)

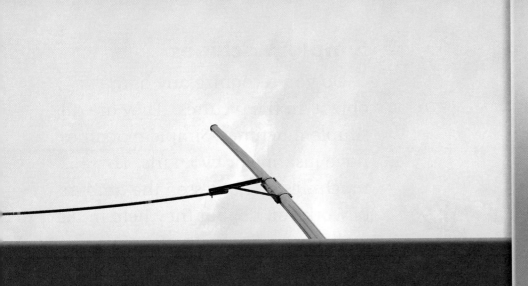

UNLOCK THE BIG ?

I will know some simple machines and how they help people do work.

Words to Know

work   inclined
wheel and   plane
    axle   pulley
wedge   screw
lever

Work

Is kicking a soccer ball work? To a scientist it is. In science, **work** means the use of a force to move an object across a distance. You do work when you rake leaves, pedal a bike, or kick a soccer ball.

It may be hard to solve a math problem. But it is not work. You may push hard to move a large rock. But it is not work if the rock does not move. You only do work when you move an object. The amount of work you do depends on how much force you use and how far you move the object.

1. ⊙ **Main Idea and Details** Complete the graphic organizer below. Write details about work.

Main Idea

Work is the use of a force to move an object across a distance.

You do work when you move an object.

Detail

Detail

Detail

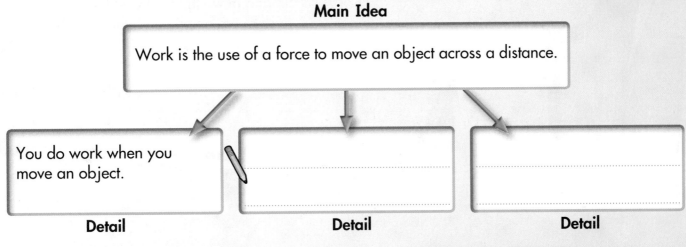

A **wheel and axle** is a round wheel attached to a post called an axle. Turning the wheel causes the axle to turn. The axle turns a small distance as the wheel turns a greater distance.

Simple Machines

Do you recognize any of the objects in the pictures? They are all simple machines. Simple machines have just one or two parts. These machines do not lessen the amount of work you do, but they help make work easier. Six kinds of simple machines help you do work. They are the wheel and axle, wedge, lever, inclined plane, pulley, and screw.

A **wedge** is a simple machine made from two slanted sides that end in a sharp edge. As a wedge is pushed through material such as wood or food, it cuts or splits the material.

2. **Identify** You want to cut a piece of cake or pie. What is the common name for the kitchen wedge you use?

....

A **lever** is a stiff bar that rests on a support. A lever is used to lift and move things. When you push down on one end, the other end lifts up.

3. Apply Look at this shape ▼. Draw an ✗ on the simple machine that has this shape. How does the shape help this machine work?

....

....

4. Identify Which simple machine would you use for each task below?

A. Raise a flag on a pole. ....

B. Pry open a can of paint. ....

C. Cut an apple. ....

A **screw** is an inclined plane wrapped around a center post. Screws can be used to hold things together and to raise and lower things.

5. Apply Tell how a jar lid is a screw.

....

A **pulley** changes the direction of motion of an object to which a force is applied. A rope pulled down on one side lifts up on the other side.

An **inclined plane,** or a ramp, is a slanted surface. It connects a lower level to a higher level. Less force is needed to move an object over a longer distance.

Complex Machines
Search your home
for one complex
machine. Draw and
label the complex
machine. Identify each
simple machine in the
complex machine.

Complex Machines

Simple machines are often put together to do bigger jobs. These complex machines are made up of simple machines that work together.

The can opener below is a complex machine. Find the simple machines that it is made of. These simple machines work together to grip, turn, and slice through a can lid.

The bicycle is a complex machine too. What simple machines make it up? How does each simple machine help make the bicycle work?

6. **Exemplify** List three complex machines that you used yesterday.

....

....

....

....

The sharp edge that cuts the top of the can is a wedge.

The winding handle is an axle that turns the gears.

The handles are made of levers.

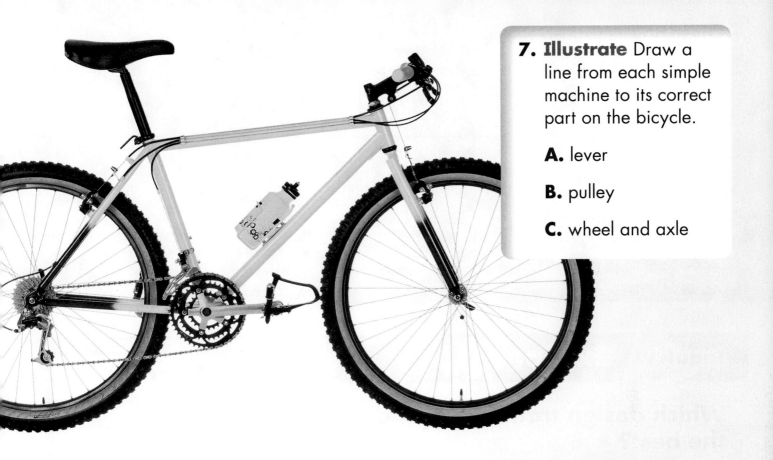

7. Illustrate Draw a line from each simple machine to its correct part on the bicycle.

A. lever

B. pulley

C. wheel and axle

Got it? 🟡 3.4.2, 3.NS.4

8. Synthesize How do you know when a simple machine has done work?

....

....

9. Summarize Write a sentence that summarizes how simple machines are useful. Give examples.

....

....

....

🔴 **Stop!** I need help with ....

⏸ **Wait!** I have a question about ....

▶ **Go!** Now I know ....

What is the design process?

Envision It!

3.DP.3 Document the design throughout the entire design process. **3.DP.4** Select a solution to the need or problem. (Also **3.DP.1, 3.DP.7, 3.DP.11**)

Tell how these two computers are different.

Inquiry **Explore It!**

Which design transfers sound the best?

☐ **1. Make a model** of a telephone. Use 2 of the cups and 3 meters of string. Thread the string through the hole in the bottom of the cup. Make a big knot.

☐ **2.** Test your model by talking into the cup. Have your partner listen. The string must be tight. **Record** how well you hear the sound.

☐ **3.** Change at least one of the cups in your model. Repeat Step 2.

Materials

2 paper, 2 plastic, and 2 foam cups (each with a hole)

string

Explain Your Results

4. Infer Which material works best for transferring sound?

3.1.1 Generate sounds using different materials, objects and techniques; record; discuss and share results. **3.DP.5** Select the most appropriate materials to develop a solution that will meet the need. **3.DP.7** Test and evaluate how well the solution meets the goal.

mysscienceonLine.com | **Explore It!** Animation

UNLOCK THE BIG ?

I will know how to conduct an investigation using the design process.

Words to know

design   prototype
  process
research

Design Process

When people design something new, they follow the steps of the design process. The **design process** is a step-by-step method used to solve a problem.

People use the design process to find a solution. A solution is an answer to a problem. The design process allows engineers to produce and test possible solutions. An engineer is any person who designs new technologies.

1. **Identify** Why is it important for engineers to follow the steps of the design process?

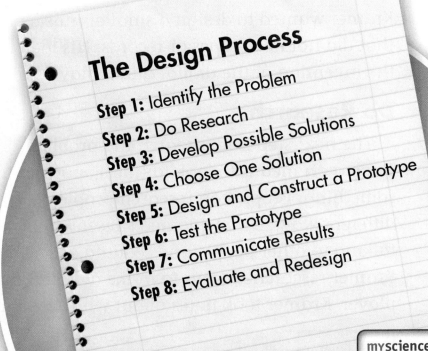

The Design Process

Step 1: Identify the Problem
Step 2: Do Research
Step 3: Develop Possible Solutions
Step 4: Choose One Solution
Step 5: Design and Construct a Prototype
Step 6: Test the Prototype
Step 7: Communicate Results
Step 8: Evaluate and Redesign

People may read books to research.

2. **Describe** How do you think Kramer researched the problem?

....

....

....

....

....

....

Identify the Problem

Engineers identify the problem during the first step of the design process. Before producing a design, engineers consider if there is a need for it. In 1979, there were only large music players that needed tapes or records to play music. British inventor Kane Kramer identified this as a problem. Kramer wanted to design a smaller music player that did not need tapes or records. His idea led to the invention of the digital audio player.

Do Research

The next step is to research the problem. **Research** means to look for facts about something. People can research problems in different ways. Some engineers research by talking to other people and reading articles. Kramer researched ways to make a digital audio player. Kramer took notes about what he learned.

Develop Possible Solutions

After doing research, engineers think of possible solutions. They consider what designs would best meet the needs of the problem. Kramer considered different materials that were available. He knew he needed to use materials that would produce a player people would use. It had to be small enough to fit in a pocket. He made different sketches of how the player could look.

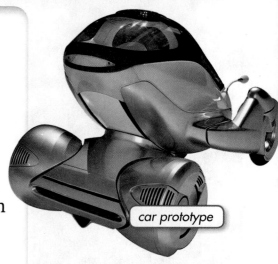

car prototype

Choose One Solution

People consider many things in order to choose the best solution. They think about how they will build the solution. They also think about what kinds of materials will work. Kramer chose the best solution. His player would be made of strong materials and be small in size.

4. Determine How can this car prototype help engineers?

Design and Construct a Prototype

After sketching the digital audio player, Kramer constructed, or built, a prototype. A **prototype** is the first working product that uses a design. Kramer made the player small and easy to use.

Someone may test an inner part of a computer to see how well it works.

Test the Prototype

Engineers test a prototype to determine if it meets their expectations. They perform multiple tests to get accurate results. Kramer tested the prototype to see how well it worked.

3. Suggest What do you think Kramer learned from his test?

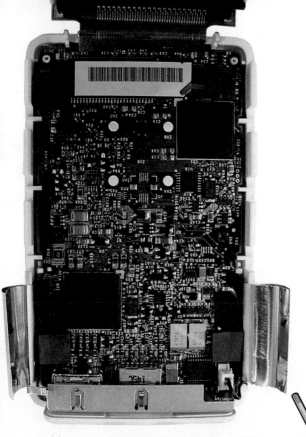

Communicate Results

Engineers communicate results about their tests to people working with them. Engineers may share how they designed and built the prototype. They also explain how the experiment was carried out. After testing it, Kramer sent a report of his invention to a group of people. He hoped the people would invest money in his invention. The report described the way his invention worked. It also explained how the player could change the way people listened to music.

5. Predict What would happen if engineers did not communicate their evidence with others?

....

....

....

This is what the inside of a digital audio player looks like. Showing it to others can help them understand the design.

Do the math!

Read a Circle Graph

Mark's digital audio player can hold 1,000 songs. Look at the circle graph below. It tells you what types of music are on Mark's player and how many songs are in each type.

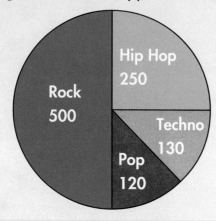

1 What type of music does Mark have the most of?

....

2 How many techno and hip hop songs does Mark have?

....

3 Solve How many more hip hop songs are there than pop songs?

....

myscienceonline.com | Got *it?* 60-Second Video

Evaluate and Redesign

The final step is to evaluate and redesign the prototype. Evaluate means to find out how well something works. People try to make a prototype better by redesigning it. When people heard about Kramer's idea of the digital audio player, they designed their own version. The first digital audio player became available to the public in 1997. It could play about one hour of music. Newer digital audio players can hold enough music to play for more than 100 days!

6. **Contrast** Look at the images to the right. How has the design process changed digital audio players?

Got it?   🕐 3.DP.1, 3.DP.3, 3.DP.4, 3.DP.7, 3.DP.11

7. **Infer** How can the design process help someone invent something?

8. **Clarify** Why is it important to test a design multiple times?

⬜ **Stop!** I need help with

⏸ **Wait!** I have a question about

▶ **Go!** Now I know

What makes a bridge strong?

Follow a Procedure

☐ **1.** Place two stacks of books 25 centimeters apart.

☐ **2. Make a model** of a bridge between the books. Use stir sticks, tape, and a note card. Brainstorm potential solutions.

☐ **3.** Place the cup on the bridge.

Materials

ruler

4 books

10 craft sticks

10 stir sticks

note card

tape

pennies

plastic cup

> **Inquiry Skill** Scientists **make a model** to help them understand how something works and predict results.

3.DP.2 Brainstorm potential solutions. **3.DP.7** Test and evaluate how well the solution meets the goal. **3.DP.9** Present evidence using mathematical representations (graphs, data tables). (Also **3.DP.5**)

☐ **4. Predict** how many pennies the bridge will hold.
Record your prediction.

☐ **5.** Put pennies in the cup one at a time. Record how
many pennies the bridge holds before it falls.

Which Bridge Is Stronger?		
Model	**Number of Pennies**	
	Prediction	**Count**
Stir sticks		
Craft sticks		

☐ **6.** Repeat Steps 2–5. Use craft sticks this time.

Analyze and Conclude

7. **Infer** How did this scientific **investigation**
help you determine which bridge was stronger?

....

....

....

8. How are your **models** like real bridges?
How are they different?

....

....

....

Air Traffic Controller

🕐 **3.DP.1**

You are in the control tower at an airport. You can see all the planes and runways. As an air traffic controller, your job is to make sure the planes take off and land safely.

Computers tell you the height, speed, and course of all the aircraft. Computers also tell how the weather is changing, minute by minute. You need to interpret this information and give pilots directions. Has the wind suddenly changed direction? Is the weather foggy, making it hard for pilots to see? Is a thunderstorm approaching? You give pilots directions to help them avoid bad weather and keep their planes a safe distance from other planes.

People who become air traffic controllers usually attend four years of college. They take classes to learn about weather and how to use equipment. What they learn helps them be good controllers.

APPLY THE BIG ?

How do you think the design process helped air traffic controllers do their job?

Vocabulary Smart Cards

technology
work
wheel and axle
wedge
lever
inclined plane
pulley
screw
design process
research
prototype

Play a Game!

Cut out the Vocabulary Smart Cards.

Cover the words on the front of each card with sticky notes.

Use the list of words above to guess which word goes with each picture. Write the word on the sticky note.

Then remove the sticky note to see if you were correct.

wedge

cuña

technology

tecnología

lever

palanca

work

trabajo

inclined plane

plano inclinado

wheel and axle

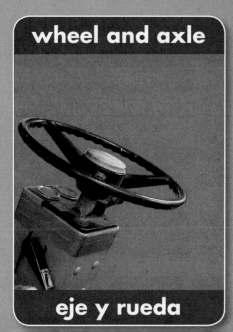

eje y rueda

use of science knowledge to invent tools and new ways of doing things

Write an example of this word.

....

....

uso del conocimiento científico para inventar instrumentos y nuevas maneras de hacer las cosas

---

two slanted sides that end in a sharp edge

Draw an example.

dos lados inclinados que terminan con un borde filoso

Interactive Vocabulary

examine
test
observe **research** study
learn
inquire

Make a Word Wheel!

Choose a vocabulary word and write it in the center of the Word Wheel graphic organizer. Write synonyms or related words on the wheel spokes.

---

the use of a force to move an object across a distance

Write a nonexample of this word.

....

....

....

uso de una fuerza para mover un objeto, por cierta distancia

---

a simple machine to lift and move things by using a stiff bar that rests on a support

List three examples of this word.

....

....

máquina simple que se usa para levantar y mover cosas mediante una barra rígida que tiene un punto de apoyo

---

a round wheel attached to a post

Draw and label a machine that has a wheel and axle.

figura circular que gira alrededor de una varilla

---

a slanting surface that connects a lower level to a higher level

Write a synonym for this word.

....

....

....

superficie inclinada que conecta un nivel bajo con un nivel más alto

70

research

hacer una investigación

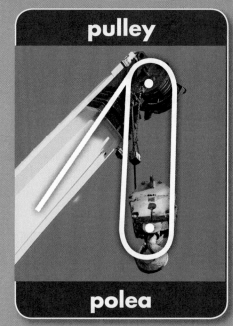

pulley

polea

prototype

prototipo

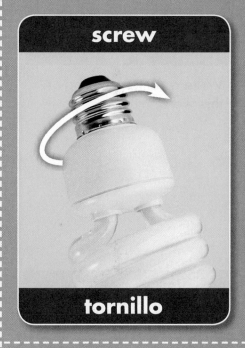

screw

tornillo

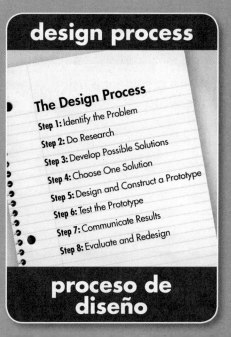

design process

The Design Process

Step 1: Identify the Problem

Step 2: Do Research

Step 3: Develop Possible Solutions

Step 4: Choose One Solution

Step 5: Design and Construct a Prototype

Step 6: Test the Prototype

Step 7: Communicate Results

Step 8: Evaluate and Redesign

proceso de diseño

a machine that changes the direction of motion of an object to which a force is applied

What is the base word in this word?

....

....

máquina que cambia la dirección en que se mueve un objeto al que se ha aplicado fuerza

---

to look for facts about something

Write three examples of research.

....

....

....

buscar datos sobre algo

---

an inclined plane wrapped around a center post

Write a sentence using this word.

....

....

....

plano inclinado enrollado alrededor de un eje central

---

the first working product that uses a design

Write a synonym for this word.

....

....

el primer producto que funciona y que sigue un diseño

---

a step-by-step method used to solve a problem

Write a sentence using this word.

....

....

....

método que sigue pasos y que se usa para resolver un problema

Lesson 1

What is technology?

- Scientific discoveries can lead to the development of new technology.
- Technology can help people solve problems.

Lesson 2

What is a machine?

- In science, work is done when a force moves an object.
- Simple machines, such as pulleys, make work easier.
- Complex machines are made of two or more simple machines.

Lesson 3

The Design Process

Step 1: Identify the Problem
Step 2: Do Research
Step 3: Develop Possible Solutic
One Solution

What is the design process?

- The design process is a step-by-step method used to solve a problem.
- People research and develop possible solutions to problems.

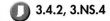
What is technology?

1. Vocabulary The use of science knowledge to invent new ways of doing things is called _____.
A. scientific methods
B. evidence
C. a tool
D. technology

2. Write about it Explain how solar panels can improve our lives. Use the word technology.

_____

_____

_____

_____

_____

_____

_____

3. Determine A Global Positioning System relies on signals sent from a(n) _____.
A. space satellite
B. X ray
C. solar panel
D. person

What is a machine?

4. Evaluate What kind of simple tool is a nail? What is one way you could use a nail?

_____

_____

_____

5. Vocabulary What machine is an inclined plane wrapped around a center post?
A. lever
B. pulley
C. wedge
D. screw

6. Classify The nail clippers are a complex machine made up of two simple machines. Label each simple machine.

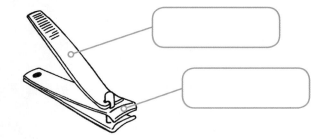

Lesson 3 *3.DP.1, 3.DP.3, 3.DP.4, 3.DP.7, 3.DP.11*

What is the design process?

7. ◉ **Main Idea and Details**
Read the selection. Then complete the graphic organizer.

> When using the design process, you can do research in many ways. You can read a newspaper. You can watch a film. You can use the Internet. It is important to do different kinds of research.

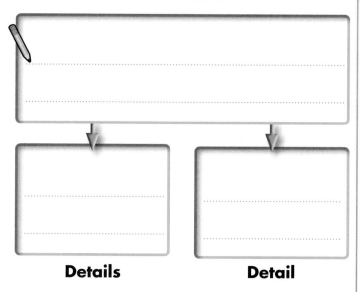

Main Idea

Details   **Detail**

8. Determine After you test a prototype, you communicate information to other people. This information is called _____.
A. a hypothesis
B. results
C. a story
D. an investigation

9. APPLY THE BIG ? **How can technology affect our lives?**

Think about a product you use. How do you think it was made? Use the vocabulary words *technology* and *design process*.

Multiple Choice

1 Which technology protects people from diseases?

A. vaccines

B. solar panel

C. Global Positioning System

D. computer chip

⟨⟩ 3.4.2, 3.DP.1

Constructed Response

2 Simple machines make doing work easier. Describe how you could use a wheel and axle.

....

....

....

....

....

....

....

⟨⟩ 3.NS.4

Extended Response

3 Jay made three different remote-controlled car prototypes. He tested each prototype for speed. His results are listed in miles per hour (mph) in the chart below.

Cars	Test 1 (mph)	Test 2 (mph)
Prototype 1	48	42
Prototype 2	53	50
Prototype 3	51	49

Which prototype went the fastest?

....

What is the difference in speed between the slowest prototype and the fastest prototype?

....

....

Why is it important for Jay to test his prototypes multiple times?

....

....

⟨⟩ 3.DP.8

Studying Clouds From Space

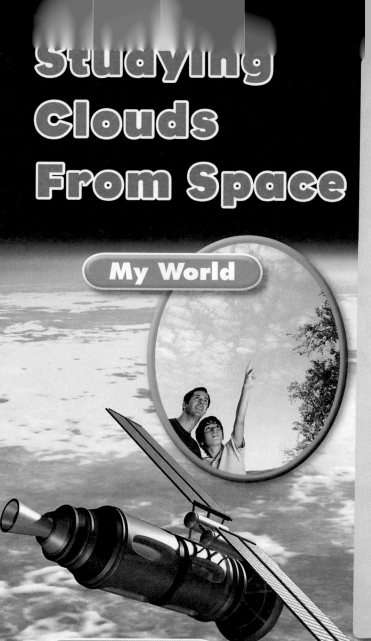

My World

Big World

3.NS.8

Did you ever lie on your back and look at the clouds? Clouds can form interesting shapes. They also can tell you things about the weather. For example, cirrus clouds are thin, feathery clouds high in the air. Cirrus clouds are a sign of fair weather. Stratus clouds cover the sky like a blanket. They often bring rain or snow.

Some scientists study clouds from space using satellites. They are trying to understand how clouds affect Earth's climate. Some satellite tools measure the sunlight that bounces off clouds. Scientists are finding that low, thick clouds reflect sunlight back into space. These clouds have a cooling effect on Earth.

Cirrus clouds are different. They allow sunlight to pass to Earth. The heat is then trapped. These clouds have a heating effect.

APPLY THE BIG ? What other examples of technology help people study the weather?

....

....

....

....

Design It!

How will you move a cargo across a river?

People have long needed to move cargo from one place to another. Sometimes there is a river in the way. Your challenge is to design a way to move cargo from one side of a river to the other side without the cargo touching the water. Your cargo is a plastic cup with 50 gram cubes. You must use at least one simple machine.

wheel and axle

wedge

pulley

inclined plane

lever

screw

Identify the problem.

☐ **1.** Identify the problems you need to solve with your **design.**

....

....

....

....

Possible Materials

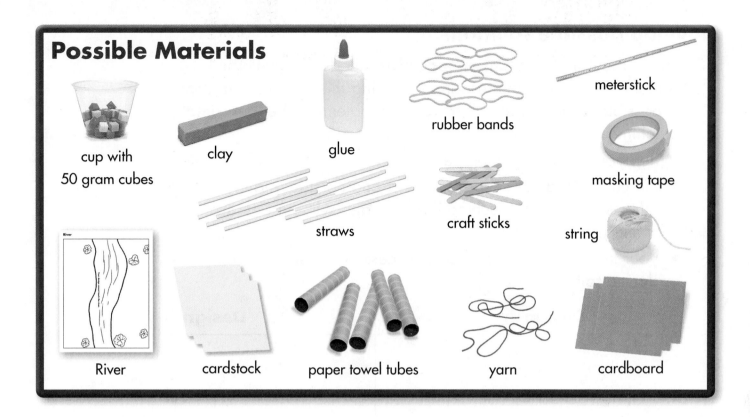

cup with
50 gram cubes

clay

glue

rubber bands

meterstick

masking tape

straws

craft sticks

string

River

cardstock

paper towel tubes

yarn

cardboard

Do research.

☐ **2.** Think about the problems you have identified.
Research **design** solutions others have used.
List 3 solutions others have used.

3.4.2 Define the uses and types of simple machines and utilize simple machines in the solution to a real world problem. **3.DP.1** Identify a need or problem to be solved. **3.DP.2** Brainstorm potential solutions. **3.DP.3** Document the design throughout the entire design process. **3.DP.4** Select a solution to the need or problem. **3.DP.5** Select the most appropriate materials to develop a solution that will meet the need. **3.DP.6** Create the solution through a prototype. **3.DP.7** Test and evaluate how well the solution meets the goal. **3.DP.8** Evaluate and test the design using measurement. **3.DP.9** Present evidence using mathematical representations (graphs, data tables). **3.DP.10** Communicate the solution including evidence using mathematical representations (graphs, data tables), drawings or prototypes. **3.DP.11** Communicate how to improve the solution.

79

Develop possible solutions.

☐ **3.** Think about the problems your **design** needs to solve. Think about the solutions you researched. Using this information, draw 2 possible designs that will solve the problems. Label any simple machines.

When you test your prototype:

- the cup with gram cubes must start on one side and end up on the other side without touching the river and without any gram cubes spilling.

- your testing is finished after 3 successful crossings or when the design fails.

Design A	Design B

Choose one solution.

☐ **4.** Choose one design to test. Tell which design you chose. Explain your choice.

....

....

....

....

Design and construct a prototype.

☐ **5.** Draw the **design** you will use to make a prototype.
Label each part. Say what it is made of.

☐ **6.** List the materials you used in your prototype.

....

....

....

Test the prototype.

☑ **7.** Test your **design.** Use 50 gram cubes.

☑ **8.** Repeat the test three times. **Record** if your design passed or failed the test.

Prototype Testing Results	
Trial	**Pass or Fail**
1	
2	
3	

Communicate results.

☑ **9.** What parts of your **design** worked in your prototype? Use the results of your trials and your **observations** to support your conclusions.

....

....

....

....

....

☐ **10.** What parts of your design could be improved? Explain.

....

....

....

....

Evaluate and redesign.

☑ **11.** Think about what did and did not work.
Use what you learned from testing to **redesign** your prototype.
Write or draw your design changes.

Master Investigator

Create a trading card for a new card game about scientific investigation. Your card will represent a scientific investigator. Describe the investigator's strengths and weaknesses. Include a question the investigator might ask to solve a problem. Compare cards to discover the best scientific investigator!

3.NS.4

Make a Model

Use paper, glue, colored markers, and other supplies to build a model of something. You can build a rocket, a car, a bridge, or anything that interests you. Describe the parts of your model and how the parts work together.

- How does your model help explain how the real object works?

- How is your model not exactly the same as the real object?

3.NS.7, 3.DP.5

Make a Poster

Make a poster that teaches about the different kinds of simple machines. Use magazine pictures that show simple machines, or draw your own pictures. Label each simple machine. Write how each simple machine helps people do work.

3.4.2

Using Scientific Methods

1. Ask a question.
2. State your hypothesis.
3. Identify and control variables.
4. Test your hypothesis.
5. Collect and record your data.
6. Interpret your data.
7. State your conclusion.
8. Go further.

Physical Science

When can you hang on to water?

Matter and Its Properties

Vertical ice climbing is challenging. Vertical ice climbing requires a lot of safety equipment. People climb ice in mountainous regions around the world, including the Rockies.

Explain What properties do you think allow climbers to climb ice? Why?

....

....

....

THE BIG ?

How can matter be described?

How can you classify objects?

Objects can be classified by listening to the sound they make when dropped.

☐ **1. Observe** Drop each object. Listen to the sound.

☐ **2.** Have one member of your group hold up a folder. Drop an object behind the folder so that others in your group cannot see.

☐ **3.** Ask them to identify the object that made the sound. Repeat with each object.

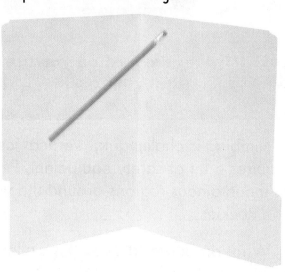

Materials

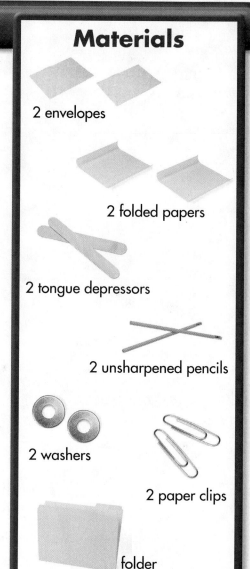

2 envelopes

2 folded papers

2 tongue depressors

2 unsharpened pencils

2 washers

2 paper clips

folder

☐ **4. Classify** Group the objects with similar sounds.

Explain Your Results

5. Classify Some objects make similar sounds. How are the objects alike?

6. **Communicate** How can you use sound to classify objects?

Inquiry Skill
Observing objects carefully can help you **classify** them.

3.1.1 Generate sounds using different materials, objects and techniques; record; discuss and share results. **3.1.3** Investigate and recognize that sound moves through solids, liquids and gases (air). (Also **3.NS.8**)

◉ Compare and Contrast

- When you **compare** things, you tell how they are alike.
- When you **contrast** things, you tell how they are different.

Rock Collectors

Ben and Misha both collect rocks. Ben likes brightly colored rocks. He is a member of a rock-hunters club. This club goes on collecting trips. Misha has a different way of collecting her favorite kinds of rocks—rocks that have fossils. Misha's uncle sends her rocks that have fossils from all around the world. Unlike Ben, Misha just has to make the trip to her mailbox to add to her collection.

Practice It!

Complete the graphic organizer to compare and contrast Ben's and Misha's favorite rocks and the way they collect rocks.

Ben   **Misha**

Lesson 1
What is matter?

3.NS.7 Keep accurate records in a notebook during investigations and communicate findings to others using graphs, charts, maps and models through oral and written reports.
(Also 3.1.3, 3.NS.1)

Envision It!

Tell how you can describe these objects.

MY PLANET DIARY

Have you heard people tell you to drink milk? Did you know milk contains a metal? Calcium is in milk. Calcium is the most common metal in your body. A substance that contains calcium is in your bones and teeth. In nature, it is also in seashells and coral. This substance that contains calcium gives bones, teeth, and seashells their strength.

bone—a substance that contains calcium and other elements

pure calcium

Why do you think your body contains a lot of calcium?

....

....

....

What do you think might happen if your body did not get enough calcium?

....

....

....

UNLOCK
THE BIG
?

I will know about
matter and some
of its properties.

Words to Know

matter   texture
property   hardness

Matter Everywhere

Everything you can see, smell, or touch is matter. Many things that you cannot see, smell, or touch are matter too. Air is an example of matter you sometimes cannot see, smell, or touch. **Matter** is anything that takes up space and has mass. You can feel the mass of objects as weight when you pick them up. When you blow up a balloon, you see that even air takes up space.

Look at the hockey puck and volleyball. The puck is small and hard. The volleyball is large and soft. The puck and volleyball look different, but they are both matter.

1. ◎ **Compare and Contrast** How are the hockey puck and the volleyball alike and different?

Hockey Puck   **Volleyball**

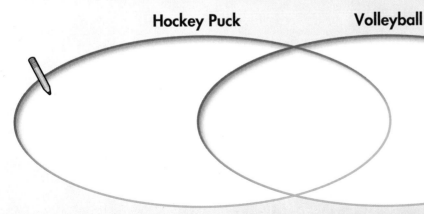

Properties of Matter

A **property** is something about matter that you can observe with one or more of your senses. Some properties of matter are size, shape, color, texture, and hardness. A basketball might be large, round, orange, bumpy, and hard. *Bumpy* and *smooth* describe an object's texture. **Texture** is how an object feels to the touch. **Hardness** describes how firm an object is.

The properties of an object depend in part on the materials it is made from. Wood, plastic, rubber, and metals are examples of materials. A tennis ball and a basketball make different sounds when they bounce off a floor. This is partly because the balls are made from different materials with different properties. Your sense of smell tells you about another property—odor.

2. **Identify** Name two materials your shoes are made from. Compare the texture of the materials.

....

....

....

....

3. **Tell** Which properties of matter best describe this flower?

Lightning Lab

"Clay Around"
Change the shape of a piece of clay. Can it be changed back? Mix the clay with clay of another color. Can it be changed back? Describe the ways the clay can be changed back. Describe the ways the clay cannot be changed back.

myscienceonline.com | Got it? | 60-Second Video

4. Look around your classroom. Write the names of four more objects. Use a different property of matter to describe each object.

Object	Property	Description
globe	shape	round
	size	
	color	
	texture	
	hardness	

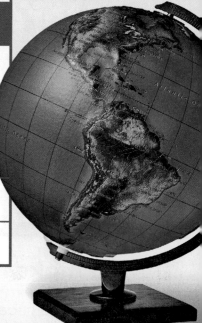

Got it? 🌓 3.1.3, 3.NS.1, 3.NS.7

5. Define What is matter?

....

....

6. ◎ **Compare and Contrast** Think about a tennis ball and a bowling ball. Compare and contrast both objects using two properties of matter.

....

....

🔲 **Stop!** I need help with ....

⏸ **Wait!** I have a question about ....

▶ **Go!** Now I know ....

What are states of matter?

Envision It!

 3.1.3 Investigate and recognize that sound moves through solids, liquids and gases (air).

Tell what you think the black rock around the flowing lava is.

Inquiry Explore It!

What makes water change states?

☐ **1.** Put an ice cube in the cup.
Put the cup into the bag. Seal the bag.

☐ **2.** Tape the bag to a sunny window.
Predict what will happen over the next day.

☐ **3. Record** your **observations.** Discuss.
Try to explain the changes you observed.

Materials

cup

ice cube

plastic bag

tape

Data Table

Time	Prediction	Observation
After 2 hours		
After 24 hours		

Explain Your Results

4. Infer   What made the ice change?

mysscienceonline.com | **Explore It!** Animation

3.NS.1 Make predictions and formulate testable questions. 3.NS.3 Plan and carry out investigations as a class, in small groups or independently, often over a period of several class lessons. (Also 3.NS.9)

UNLOCK
THE BIG ?

I will know three states of matter. I will know how water changes states.

Words to Know

states of matter   boil
freeze   evaporation
melt   condensation

States of Matter

All matter is made of small particles. These particles are so small that you cannot see them, even under a magnifying lens. The particles are always moving. In some kinds of matter, the particles are held tightly together. In other kinds of matter, they are held less tightly.

States of matter are the forms that matter can take. Three states of matter are solids, liquids, and gases. In solids, particles are held tightly together. In liquids, particles are held together less tightly. In gases, particles move about freely.

Your science book is a solid. Like other solids, the book does not change shape. The particles of solids are held tightly together.

1. **Circle** the words that name the three states of matter.

2. **Explain** Which objects in your backpack are solids? How do you know?

....

....

....

....

Change of States

Get two cups. Fill each cup with the same amount of water. Mark the water level. Put one cup in a freezer. Put the other cup on a shelf. Observe what happens to the level of water in each cup after three hours.

The illustrations in the circles show how particles are arranged in solids, liquids, and gases.

Solids

Solids are made of tightly packed particles. Solids have their own shape. You can easily measure both the mass and the volume of solids. Like your science book, the fabric of the balloons and balloon baskets in the picture are also solids. The particles in the fabric of the balloon and baskets are tightly packed together.

3. Tell two other solids you see in the picture.

Liquids

Particles in liquids are held together less tightly. The particles in a liquid flow past one another. Liquids take the shape of their containers. If you pour a liquid from one container to another, the liquid will take the shape of the new container. You can easily measure the mass and volume of liquids.

Gases

The tiny particles that make up gas are far apart compared to solids and liquids. The particles of a gas move freely and take up the space of their container. The particles of a gas bounce off one another as they move freely. All matter has mass, so gas has mass too. You can measure the mass and volume of a gas.

The air in the balloon is a gas. The air takes the shape of this balloon. The particles of air move freely in the balloon.

4. [CHALLENGE] Other than balloons, what objects give gases a different shape? Explain.

....

....

Changes in Water

Matter can change states through heating or cooling. When water heats up, the space between the water particles becomes greater. When water cools down, the space between the water particles becomes less.

When liquid water cools to 0°C (32°F), it **freezes,** or changes from a liquid to a solid. It changes to ice, solid water. When ice is heated, it **melts,** or changes from a solid to a liquid. Ice melts at 0°C (32°F).

You can see water as a liquid and as a solid. You cannot see water as a gas. Water as a gas is called *water vapor.* When water is heated to 100°C, it **boils,** or changes from liquid water into bubbles of water vapor. Water vapor and steam are not the same. Steam is droplets of liquid water in the air.

When water boils, it evaporates. **Evaporation** is the change from liquid water to water vapor. Evaporation can also happen slowly at the water's surface.

5. **Explain** Tell what state of matter water changes into when it evaporates.

6. [CHALLENGE] What do the melting temperature and freezing temperature of water have in common?

condensation

myscienceonline.com | Got it? 60-Second Video

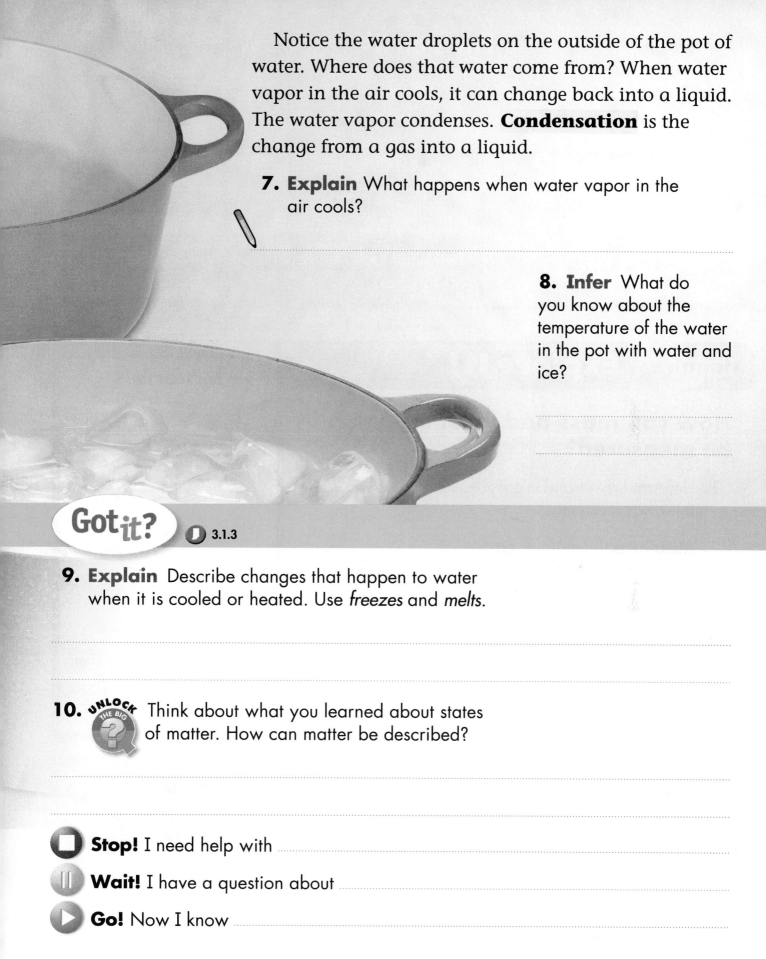

Notice the water droplets on the outside of the pot of water. Where does that water come from? When water vapor in the air cools, it can change back into a liquid. The water vapor condenses. **Condensation** is the change from a gas into a liquid.

7. **Explain** What happens when water vapor in the air cools?

8. **Infer** What do you know about the temperature of the water in the pot with water and ice?

Got it? ◐ 3.1.3

9. **Explain** Describe changes that happen to water when it is cooled or heated. Use *freezes* and *melts*.

10. **UNLOCK THE BIG ?** Think about what you learned about states of matter. How can matter be described?

⬛ **Stop!** I need help with

⫴ **Wait!** I have a question about

▶ **Go!** Now I know

How is matter measured?

3.4.1 Choose and use the appropriate tools to estimate and measure length, mass and temperature in SI units. 3.NS.5 Use measurement skills and apply appropriate units when collecting data.

Tell what tools you could use to measure the art supplies.

Inquiry **Explore It!**

How can mass and volume be measured?

☐ **1.** Hold an eraser and a crayon. Tell which you think has more mass.

☐ **2.** **Measure** the mass of each. Use a balance. **Record.**

_____ g   _____ g
(eraser)   (crayon)

☐ **3.** Look at each liquid. **Predict** which has the greater volume.

☐ **4.** Measure the volume of each liquid. Use the graduated cylinder. Record.

_____ mL   _____ mL
(red liquid)   (blue liquid)

Explain Your Results

5. Tell how mass and volume can be **measured**.

_____

_____

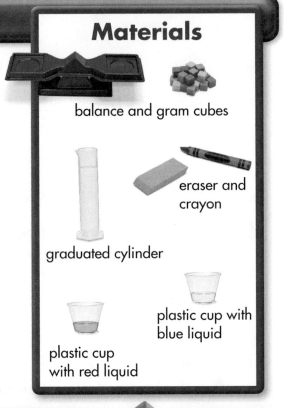

Materials

balance and gram cubes

eraser and crayon

graduated cylinder

plastic cup with blue liquid

plastic cup with red liquid

myscienceonline.com | **Explore It!** Animation

3.NS.1 Make predictions and formulate testable questions. (Also **3.NS.4**)

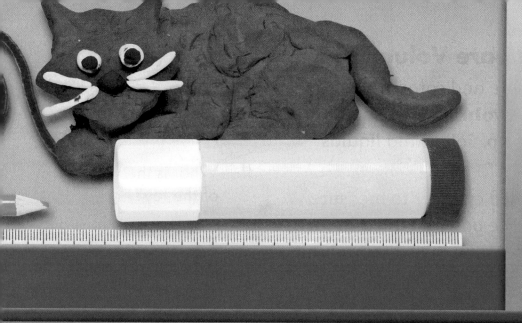

UNLOCK
THE BIG
?

I will know how to measure and compare properties of matter.

Words to Know

volume
mass

Measure Length

Matter is anything that has mass and takes up space. Length is one property of matter that can be measured. Length is the distance from one end of an object to the other end. To measure length, you can use metric rulers and metersticks. You can use these lengths to compare objects. For example, you can measure and compare the length of a pillbug and a beetle to determine which one is longer.

The basic metric unit of length is the meter (m). Shorter lengths are measured in centimeters (cm) or millimeters (mm). There are 100 cm in a meter. There are 1,000 mm in a meter. Longer distances are measured in kilometers (km). There are 1,000 m in a kilometer.

1. **Solve** Some objects are too small to see easily. A hand lens or magnifying glass makes this pillbug easier to measure. Measure about how long this pillbug is in centimeters.

....

....

Measure and Compare Volume

Another way to measure and compare matter is by volume. An object's **volume** is the amount of space the object takes up. Solids and liquids have volume.

You can use a graduated cylinder to measure the volume of a liquid. The basic metric unit for measuring liquid volume is the liter (L). Graduated cylinders mark smaller parts of a liter called milliliters (mL). There are 1,000 milliliters in a liter.

You can measure the volume of a solid, like a rock, using water. A rock keeps its shape in water. A rock pushes water out of its way when it sinks.

2. Solve Compare the volume of the toy to the volume of the rock.

What is the volume of the toy?

What is the volume of the rock?

Which object has a greater volume?

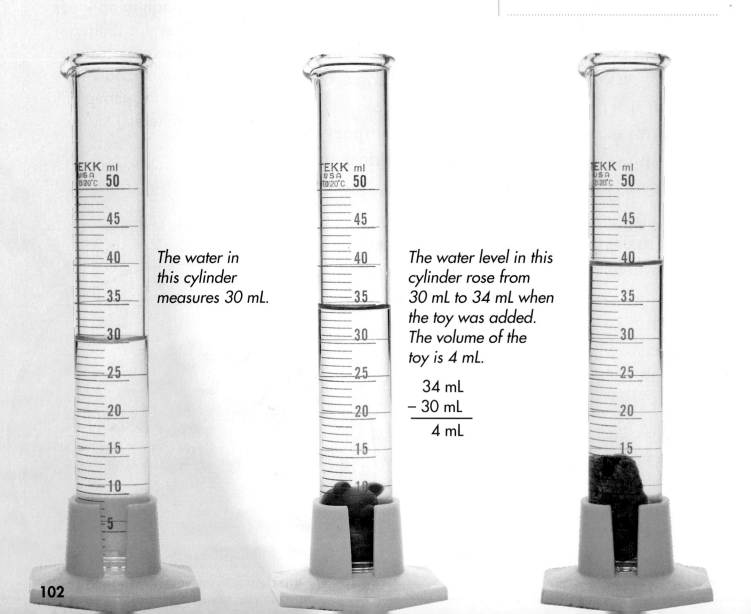

The water in this cylinder measures 30 mL.

The water level in this cylinder rose from 30 mL to 34 mL when the toy was added. The volume of the toy is 4 mL.

$$34 \text{ mL}$$
$$- 30 \text{ mL}$$
$$\overline{4 \text{ mL}}$$

Measure and Compare Mass

You can also measure an object's mass. An object's **mass** is the amount of matter it has. Solids, liquids, and gases all have mass. A balance is a tool used to measure mass.

A metric unit for mass is the gram (g). Larger matter is measured in kilograms (kg). There are 1,000 grams in a kilogram.

3. Solve What is the mass of the crayon?

Lightning Lab

Volume and Mass
Use a funnel. Fill a balloon with sand. Fill another balloon with an equal volume of water. Tie each balloon closed. Measure and compare the mass of each balloon.

Each cube has a mass of 1 g.

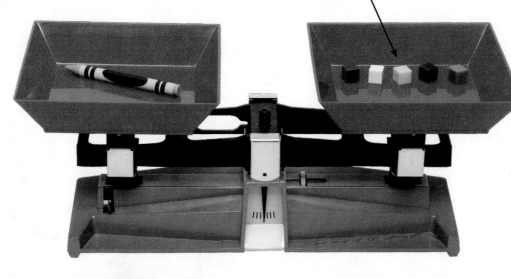

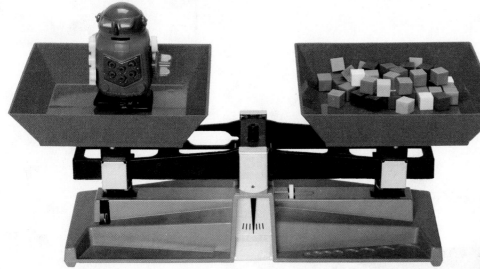

4. Solve The balance pans containing the robot and gram cubes below are even. There are 52 cubes on one pan. What is the mass of the robot?

5. Compare Which has greater mass—the crayon or robot?

Problem Solving

Common Objects	Mass (g)
stapler	500
paper clip	1
pencil	5
dime	2

1 List the objects in the chart in order from least mass to greatest mass.

For exercises **2** through **6,** write and solve a number sentence.

2 How many dimes are needed to equal the mass of six pencils?

3 A lime has a mass of 80 grams. How many pencils are needed to equal the mass of one lime?

4 A mug has a mass of 400 grams. How many more grams does a stapler have than a mug?

5 You have nine dimes for a total mass of 18 grams. How many more grams do nine dimes have than seven paper clips?

6 An adult male killer whale has a mass of about 4,500 kg. A dictionary has a mass of 1 kg. How many dictionaries are needed to equal the mass of an adult killer whale?

Measure and Compare Temperature

You can use different scales to measure temperature. The Celsius scale is often used in science. Degrees Celsius is written as °C. The Fahrenheit scale is often used in everyday life in the United States. For example, the outside temperature is reported in degrees Fahrenheit. Degrees Fahrenheit is written as °F. Sometimes both scales are used.

6. Measure What is the temperature of the ice water in the top glass in degrees Celsius? Record the temperature next to the glass.

7. Compute The temperature of the ice in the bottom glass is 0°C (32°F). What is the temperature difference between the water in the two glasses? Show your work.

Got it?

🖉 3.4.1, 3.NS.5

8. Reconstruct How can you use a graduated cylinder to measure and compare the volume of an eraser and a paper clip?

....

....

....

9. Analyze What are you measuring when you measure an object's mass?

....

⬛ **Stop!** I need help with ....

⏸ **Wait!** I have a question about ....

▶ **Go!** Now I know ....

Inquiry Investigate It!

Does the method you use to measure affect your results?

Follow a Procedure

Using a Metric Ruler

☐ **1.** Stack ten cubes.

☐ **2.** Practice **estimating.** Estimate the height, length, and width of the stack.

_____ cm   _____ cm   _____ cm
  height   length   width

☐ **3. Measure** the height, length, and width of the stack. **Record** your measurement in the chart below.

☐ **4.** Multiply to find the volume. Record.

volume = height × length × width

☐ **5.** Repeat with the clay block. First estimate, then measure.

_____ cm   _____ cm   _____ cm
  height   length   width

volume = height × length × width

Materials

metric ruler

graduated cylinder

water

gram cubes

clay block

Inquiry Skill Scientists **measure** carefully and record data accurately.

Measuring Volume Using a Metric Ruler

	Height (cm)	**Length** (cm)	**Width** (cm)	**Volume** (cm³)
Stack of gram cubes	_____	_____	_____	_____
Clay block	_____	_____	_____	_____

3.4.1 Choose and use the appropriate tools to estimate and measure length, mass and temperature in SI units. **3.DP.9** Present evidence using mathematical representations (graphs, data tables). (Also **3.NS.7**)

Using a Graduated Cylinder

☐ **6.** Pour 30 mL of water into the cylinder.

☐ **7.** Drop in 10 cubes one by one. Measure the volume. Record.

☐ **8.** Subtract to find the volume of the cubes. Record.

☐ **9.** Repeat with the clay block.

volume of water and object (Step 6)	_____ mL
− volume of water (Step 5)	− 30 mL
volume of object (Step 7)	_____ mL

Measuring Volume Using a Graduated Cylinder				
Object	Volume of Water with Object	Volume of Water	Volume of Object (mL)	Volume of Object (cm³) (1 cm³=1 mL)
Stack of gram cubes	_____ mL	30 mL	_____ mL	_____ cm³
Clay block	_____ mL	30 mL	_____ mL	_____ cm³

Analyze and Conclude

10. You **measured** the volume of the stack of cubes two ways. Compare your results. Were they the same? Explain.

....

....

....

11. **UNLOCK THE BIG ?** Describe the volume of solid matter.

....

....

3.NS.1

Chemist

Some chemists do experiments with plastics, which can be made from different substances.

Do you like to bake? You might not want to eat all the ingredients in bread separately. After the flour, water, and yeast are mixed and baked, however, they change. Then bread tastes just right. When you bake you use chemistry. Chemistry is the study of substances and how they change.

Chemists study the properties of substances. Some materials mix together easily. Sugar dissolves in water quickly. Other substances such as oil and water do not mix well together.

To become a chemist, students attend college and study chemistry. When they finish college they can work for many different companies or universities. Some chemists work to develop new drugs to treat diseases. Other chemists do experiments with baking products to make new foods or with crops to help them survive droughts better.

Why do you think it is important for scientists to study the properties of substances?

Vocabulary Smart Cards

matter
property
texture
hardness
states of matter
freeze
melt
boil
evaporation
condensation
volume
mass

Play a Game!

Choose a Vocabulary Smart Card.

Work with a partner. Write several sentences using the vocabulary word.

Have your partner repeat with another Vocabulary Smart Card.

hardness

dureza

matter

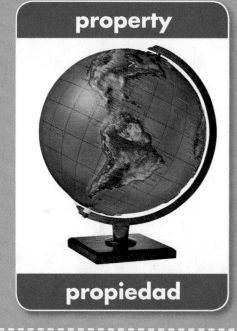

materia

states of matter

estados de la materia

property

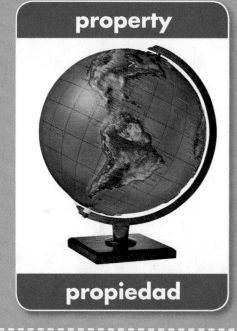

propiedad

freeze

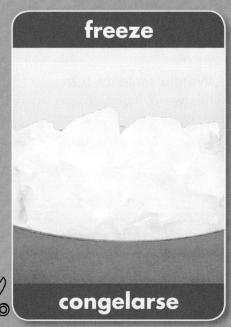

congelarse

texture

textura

Interactive Vocabulary

anything that takes up space and has mass

Write a sentence using this word.

todo lo que ocupa espacio y tiene masa

---

a description of how firm an object is

Write the adjective form of this word. Use it in a sentence.

descripción de la firmeza de un objeto

---

something about matter that you can observe with one or more of your senses

What is another meaning of this word?

algo en la materia que puedes percibir con uno o más de tus sentidos

---

forms that matter can take

Draw an example.

formas que la materia puede tener

---

how an object feels to the touch

Write a sentence using this word.

cómo se siente un objeto al tocarlo

---

to change from a liquid to a solid

Write a sentence using this word.

cambiar de líquido a sólido

Make a Word Wheel!

matter   solid   gas   liquid

Choose a vocabulary word and write it in the center of the Word Wheel graphic organizer. Write synonyms or related words on the wheel spokes.

110

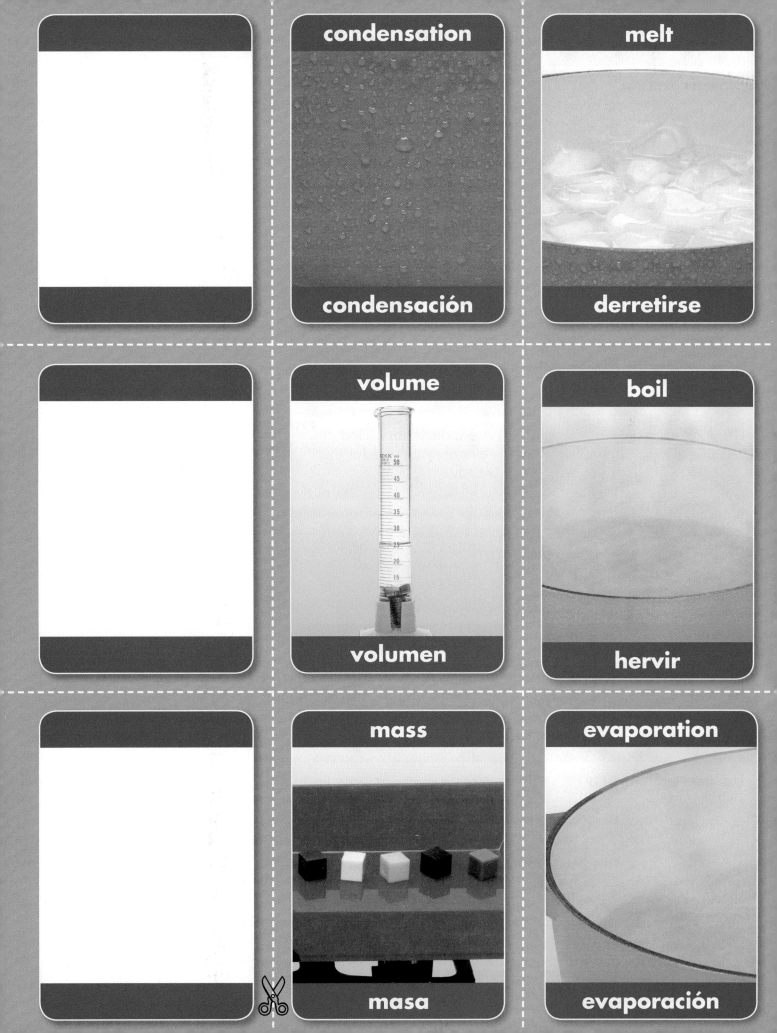

condensation

condensación

melt

derretirse

volume

volumen

boil

hervir

mass

masa

evaporation

evaporación

to change from a solid to a liquid	the change from a gas into a liquid	
Draw an example.	Write a sentence using this word.	
cambiar de sólido a líquido	cambio de estado gaseoso a líquido	

to change from liquid water into bubbles of water vapor	the amount of space an object takes up	
Draw an example.	Use a dictionary. Find several synonyms for this word.	
cambiar de agua en estado líquido a burbujas de vapor	cantidad de espacio ocupada por un objeto	

the change from liquid water to water vapor	the amount of matter an object has	
Use the verb form in a sentence.	Write a sentence using this word.	
cambio de agua en estado líquido a vapor	cantidad de materia que un objeto tiene	

Lesson 1

What is matter?

- Matter is anything that takes up space and has mass.
- Properties of matter include size, shape, color, texture, and hardness.

Lesson 2

What are states of matter?

- Three states of matter are solids, liquids, and gases.
- Water melts, freezes, boils, evaporates, and condenses.

Lesson 3

How is matter measured?

- Properties of matter, such as mass, volume, length, and temperature, can be measured and compared using tools.

Lesson 1   3.1.3, 3.NS.1, 3.NS.7
What is matter?

1. **Vocabulary** Anything that takes up space and has mass is called

   _____.

   A. water
   B. air
   C. solid
   D. matter

2. **Compare** A puzzle piece and checker pieces have different properties. Use some properties of matter to compare them.

3. **Determine** Which of your senses can you use to describe several properties of a strawberry?

Lesson 2   3.1.3
What are states of matter?

4. **Summarize** What terms did you learn that describe the changes water undergoes when it changes states through heating?

5. **Describe** What happens when water vapor comes in contact with a cold surface?

6. **Compare and Contrast** Compare and contrast water as a liquid and water as a gas.

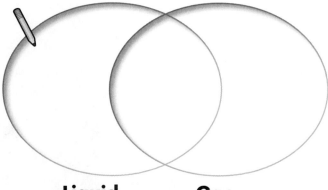

Liquid　　　**Gas**

Lesson 3 3.4.1, 3.NS.5

How is matter measured?

Do the math!

7. A drink comes in a bottle with a volume of 473 mL. The serving size on each bottle is 240 mL. Is 473 mL enough for you and your friend to each have a full serving? If not, how many milliliters short of two full servings is the bottle?

....

....

....

8. Analyze Which tool and unit of measure would you use to measure the length of a book?

....

....

....

Do the math!

9. Use the two cylinders to answer the question. What is the volume of the bolt in milliliters?

....

....

10. APPLY THE BIG ? How can matter be described?

....

Think about a calculator. How would you describe and measure it? Use the terms *state of matter* and *mass*.

....

....

....

....

....

....

Multiple Choice

1 Ice melting into water is a change between which two states of matter?

A. liquid to gas

B. solid to liquid

C. gas to liquid

D. liquid to solid

3.1.3

Constructed Response

2 Tools help to measure matter. Describe how you could measure the volume of milk in a glass. Be sure to include what tools you would use.

....

....

....

....

3.4.1

Extended Response

3 Dakota wanted to compare the mass of three cups filled with water. All three cups were the same size and had eight ounces of water in them. Each cup was made of a different material. She used a balance to find the mass in each cup. Her results are shown in the chart below.

Cup Material	Mass (grams)
Plastic	255
Metal	311
Glass	397

Which cup has the smallest mass?

....

How much more mass does the glass cup have than the metal cup?

....

Why do you think each cup has a different mass?

....

....

....

....

3.4.1

Rubber

Did you know that some or all of the rubber used to make the basketball you play with comes from as far away as Brazil or Malaysia?

Farmers collect rubber from rubber trees on farms. First, a small piece of tree bark is cut off. Then rubber flows out of the tree and is collected in containers. When rubber is first collected from trees, it's called latex. At factories, the latex is used to make sheets of rubber. Sheets of rubber are made by adding acid. Then the water is pressed out. After pressing, the sheets of rubber are sent to companies all over the world to make different things. One item made from rubber is a basketball. Most basketballs are made up of both rubber and leather.

Big World

My World

APPLY THE BIG ? What is one property you think rubber has? How do you think this property helps a basketball bounce?

....

....

....

117

How can energy keep you running?

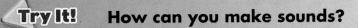

Forms of Energy

Chapter
4

Try It! How can you make sounds?

Investigate It! What makes sound change?

When was the last time you took a long run?
Running on sand takes a lot of energy. It takes
more energy to run on sand than to run on a
paved surface.

 Predict How does this runner use energy?

....

....

....

THE BIG ? How can energy change?

How can you make sounds?

☐ **1.** Make one end of a straw flat.

☐ **2.** Cut this end to look like the picture below.

☐ **3.** Put the flat end of the straw in your mouth so the cut you made is covered. Blow.

☐ **4. Observe** What does it sound like?

_____

☐ **5.** Cut 3 centimeters off the other end of the straw.

☐ **6.** Blow and describe how the sound changed.

_____

☐ **7.** Repeat Steps 5 and 6.

_____

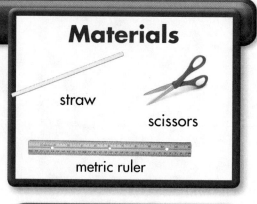

Materials

straw

scissors

metric ruler

Inquiry Skill
You can use what you **observe** to infer.

Explain Your Results

8. **UNLOCK THE BIG ?** **Infer** Explain the relationship between the length of the straw and the sound it made.

_____

_____

3.1.1 Generate sounds using different materials, objects and techniques; record; discuss and share results. **3.1.2** Investigate how the loudness and pitch of sound changes when the rate of vibrations changes. **3.NS.8** Identify simple patterns in data and propose explanations to account for the patterns.

◉ Cause and Effect

- A **cause** makes something happen.
- An **effect** is what happens.
- Science writers often use clue words and phrases such as *makes, if,* and *as a result* to signal cause and effect.

Boiling Water

If enough energy is added to liquid water, the water boils. It becomes the invisible gas called water vapor. At a temperature of 100°C (212°F), liquid water boils. Energy added at the bottom of a container makes water at the bottom change into a gas. The gas forms bubbles that are lighter than the water around them. As a result, the bubbles of gas float to the water's surface. These bubbles break open and release hot water vapor into the air.

Practice It!

Complete the graphic organizer. Use it to identify a cause and effect in the above paragraph.

Cause

Effect

What is energy?

Envision It!

3.1.6 Describe evidence to support the idea that light and sound are forms of energy. (Also 3.1.1, 3.1.3, 3.NS.3)

Circle any place you see energy in this picture.

my planet Diary

by Maddie
Wesley Chapel, Florida

I use a lot of energy because it makes my life easier. However, I try to be responsible and use less energy.

I also turn off the lights when I leave a room. Sometimes I want the lights on. Instead, I open the blinds, so I do not waste energy.

by Jordyn
Daytona Beach, Florida

Hi, Maddie. My family and I are also committed to using less energy. I turn off my fan and my radio before I go to school.

I save more energy at school. Whenever our class leaves the room, we turn off the lights. It would save a lot of energy if every class in the school did that!

Let's Blog!

Describe If you could blog back to Maddie and Jordyn, what would you blog about saving energy?

I will know energy takes many forms, causes motion, and creates change.

Words to Know
....

energy   sound energy
electrical   potential
   energy   energy
mechanical   kinetic
   energy   energy

Energy

Energy is the ability to do work or to cause change. Work is done when a force moves an object. The sun is the main source of energy at Earth's surface. Energy from the sun causes many effects. Energy from the sun makes Earth a place where we can live. Light from the sun helps plants grow. Energy from the sun causes winds to blow and water to move through the water cycle.

Energy from the sun causes lettuce to grow.

1. **◎ Cause and Effect** Complete the graphic organizer below. Write three effects of the sun's energy.

Cause	Effects
Energy from the sun	1. Plants grow.
	2. ....
	3. ....

Energy at Home

You use many forms of energy every day in your home. The living and nonliving things in the home below use many forms of energy.

Electrical energy is the movement of electric charges. It powers things that use electricity, such as a lamp.

2. Circle things that use electrical energy.

Light energy is energy we can see. Light energy comes through windows and brightens rooms.

Heat is the transfer of energy from one place to another. Heat is used to cook food in the kitchen.

3. Describe Tell how the grass growing outside of the house is evidence that light is a form of energy.

Mechanical energy is energy that motion or position gives to an object. You use mechanical energy every time you use a machine, such as a toothbrush.

4. List What four machines in the home use mechanical energy?

....

....

....

Sound energy is energy we can hear. Musical instruments produce sound energy.

5. Describe How is a vibrating guitar string evidence that sound is a form of energy?

....

....

....

6. Label Place an X on things that produce sound energy.

7. Draw Look at the house. Draw an item in the house and label the form of energy it uses.

Stored Energy

Energy can be stored. As you stand ready to jump, run, or snowboard, your body has stored energy. Stored energy makes movement possible. Stored energy is **potential energy.** Potential energy changes into another kind of energy if you use it to do work or cause a change.

A raised object has potential energy due to gravity. For example, the snowboarder at the top of the hill has potential energy because of his high position. Potential energy is also gained from stretching or compressing objects. For example, you can stretch or compress a spring to store potential energy.

The stored energy in food, fuels, and batteries is chemical energy. Stored chemical energy can change into a form that can do work. For example, the stored energy in food is released to help you move. It can also keep your body warm.

At-Home Lab

Make Motion
Get a bowl and a table tennis ball. Put the ball in the bowl. Move the bowl around. Tell how the ball moves. Tell where the ball has the most potential energy. Tell where it has the least potential energy.

8. **List** Look again at the illustration on the previous pages. List two examples of potential energy in the home.

....

....

....

9. **Describe** How do you use the stored chemical energy in batteries?

....

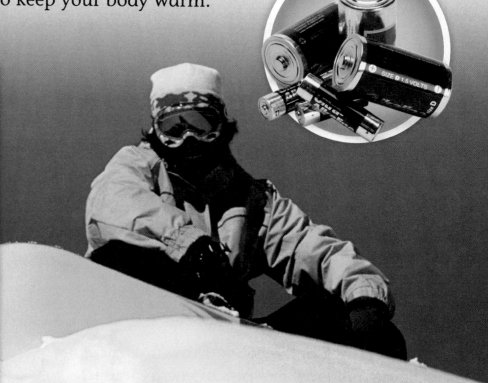

Energy of Motion

The snowboarder's potential energy due to gravity changes to kinetic energy.

Potential energy can change to **kinetic energy,** or the energy of motion. A car moves when the chemical energy stored in gasoline changes to kinetic energy. Potential energy changes to kinetic energy when you release a stretched spring. The potential energy the snowboarder has at the top of the hill changes to kinetic energy as he moves down the hill. He moves down the hill because gravity pulls him.

Some sources of energy can be replaced. After snowboarding, the snowboarder can go back up the hill to replace the potential energy he used. You can replace the potential energy of a spring by stretching or compressing it again.

10. Underline the words that tell about kinetic energy.

Got it?

3.1.1, 3.1.3, 3.1.6, 3.NS.3

11. Identify Write one way each type of energy is used.

Electrical energy ....

Mechanical energy ....

Sound energy ....

12. Explain How can the potential energy of a pencil resting on a desk change into kinetic energy?

....

....

....

Stop! I need help with ....

Wait! I have a question about ....

Go! Now I know ....

Lesson 2

What are some ways energy changes form?

3.1.3 Investigate and recognize that sound moves through solids, liquids and gases (air). (Also **3.NS.1**)

Envision It!

Tell how you think energy changes form as this electric train travels.

Inquiry Explore It!

How can sound energy change form?

☐ **1.** Add water to the sound-wave collector. Make sure the water is level with the middle of the bobber.

☐ **2.** Have another student make a loud, long, low sound straight down into the top cup. At the same time, **observe** the bobber and water. **Record** what you observe.

Materials

sound-wave collector   water

Explain Your Results

3. Communicate Think about what you **observed. Infer** how sound energy caused motion.

myscienceonline.com | **Explore It!** Animation

3.1.1 Generate sounds using different materials, objects and techniques; record; discuss and share results. **3.1.6** Describe evidence to support the idea that light and sound are forms of energy. (Also **3.1.2**, **3.NS.4**, **3.NS.8**)

UNLOCK
THE BIG
?

I will know energy can
change into many forms.

Word to Know
....
wave

Changing Forms of Energy

There are different forms of energy. Energy can change from one form to another. People change energy into forms they can easily use. For example, a music player changes electrical energy into sound energy.

Your body changes energy into forms that are useful for you. For example, your body stores potential energy from food as chemical energy. The chemical energy stored in your body changes to kinetic energy as you move.

1. (Circle) five forms of energy in the paragraphs above.

2. **Predict** Into what form of energy does this robot dog change electrical energy?

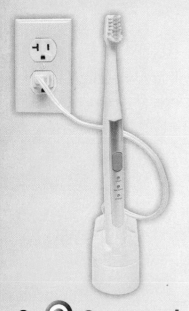

Using Energy

Sometimes people use machines to change forms of energy. You use kinetic energy to turn on a light switch, a common machine. When the light switch is turned on, electrical energy changes to light energy. A cable car, another machine, changes potential energy to kinetic energy.

An electric toothbrush is another machine. It has an electric cord that plugs into an outlet. Electrical energy is stored as chemical energy in the battery of the toothbrush. The chemical energy changes back to electrical energy when the toothbrush is turned on. The electrical energy then changes to kinetic energy as the toothbrush moves.

Energy does not change completely from one form to another. After energy is used, it does not go away, either. Some energy is always given off in the form of heat. After you turn on a light bulb, it becomes warm. This is because some of the energy becomes heat.

3.  **Cause and Effect** How could turning on this electric toothbrush produce heat?

....

....

....

4. **Hypothesize** How do you think the cable car gains potential energy?

....

....

Go Green

Reduce Energy Usage

Gasoline contains a form of stored energy. It is made from oil. There is a limited supply of oil on Earth. Think of some ways people use gasoline. Tell three ways people could use less gasoline.

How Energy Travels

Energy can travel from one place to another. Suppose a moving object strikes another object. Some kinetic energy passes to the second object. Have you ever gone bowling? When the bowling ball hits the group of pins, the ball slows down and the pins begin moving. Before hitting the pins, the bowling ball has all of the kinetic energy. The pins have no kinetic energy. When the ball hits the pins, some kinetic energy transfers to the pins. Some energy is also lost as heat. The total amount of energy does not change.

5. Underline one cause and (circle) one effect in the paragraph.

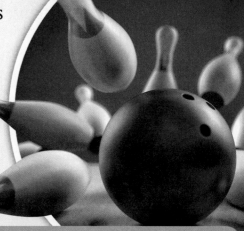

Do the math!

Model and Apply Division

Bowling requires energy. When the ball hits the pins, energy transfers from the ball to the pins. This knocks them down.

Example

In bowling, you roll a ball about 18 meters down the lane to hit the pins. If a bowling ball is thrown at 6 meters per second, how long does it take to hit the pins?

Rule: Time = Distance ÷ Speed

You can use repeated subtraction to find how many groups of 6 are in 18.

18 – 6 = 12   You can subtract 6 three times. There are three groups of 6 in 18.

12 – 6 = 6

6 – 6 = 0   The ball takes 3 seconds to hit the pins.

1 Solve If you throw the bowling ball at 3 meters per second, about how long will it take for the ball to hit the pins?

2 Hypothesize If you roll the ball too slowly, what might happen when it reaches the pins?

Waves

Energy can travel as waves. For example, light and sound travel as waves. A **wave** is a disturbance that carries energy from one point to another point. Waves of energy can look like the wave of moving rope below. The rope goes from one side of the dotted line to the other. Energy causes this effect as it travels from one end of the rope to the other.

6. ⊙ **Main Idea and Details** Read the paragraph. Write the main idea.

....

....

....

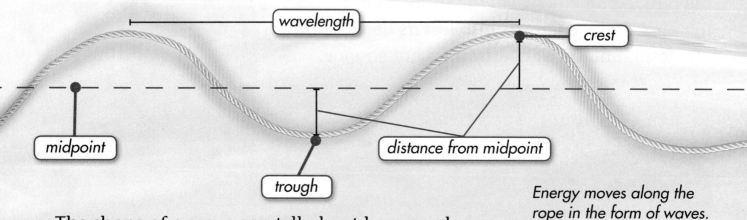

wavelength

crest

midpoint

distance from midpoint

trough

Energy moves along the rope in the form of waves.

The shape of a wave can tell about how much energy it carries. The wavelength and the distance from the midpoint to the crest or trough can indicate about how much energy a wave carries.

The bottom of a wave is called a trough. The top of a wave is called a crest. Waves with greater distance from the midpoint to a crest or trough have more energy than waves with lesser distance.

Wavelength is the distance between one crest and the next crest or one trough and the next trough. Waves with shorter wavelengths have more energy than waves with longer wavelengths.

7. **Produce** Draw a wave that carries less energy than the rope above.

Waves in water can be small, like the ripples in the bucket below. Waves caused by hurricanes can be huge! The size of a wave depends on how much energy it carries. The energy a wave carries can change. Look at the bucket. First, the energy from the falling drop disturbs the water surface. Then, as the waves move away from the source, they carry less energy.

Got it?

🕐 3.1.3, 3.NS.1

8. **Infer** How can the transfer of energy cause motion?

....

....

9. **UNLOCK THE BIG ?** Think about what you learned in this lesson. How can energy change?

....

....

....

⬛ **Stop!** I need help with ....

⏸ **Wait!** I have a question about ....

▶ **Go!** Now I know ....

How do light and matter interact?

3.1.4 Investigate how light travels through the air and tends to maintain its direction until it interacts with some other object or material. 3.1.5 Observe and describe how light is absorbed, changes its direction, is reflected back, or passes through objects. Observe and describe that when light cannot pass through an object a shadow results. (Also 3.1.6, 3.NS.1)

Envision It!

Tell where you think light is coming from in these sea jellies.

What happens when light is reflected in many directions?

☐ **1.** Shine the flashlight through the water. **Observe** the water from all directions. **Record** what you see.

....

....

☐ **2.** Add one spoonful of milk. Stir. Repeat Step 1.

....

....

Materials

flashlight

milk

spoon

clear plastic cup with water

Explain Your Results

3. Compare your **observations** before and after the milk was added.

....

....

....

myscienceonline.com | **Explore It!** Animation

3.NS.4 Perform investigations using appropriate tools and technology that will extend the senses.

I will know how objects reflect, refract, and absorb light. I will know how light forms shadows.

Words to Know
....

light energy   absorb
reflect   shadow
refract

Path of Light

You can see objects because of light energy. **Light energy** is energy we can see. Light travels outward from its source in all directions. Light travels in straight lines until it strikes an object or travels from one medium to another. For example, light from a light bulb can brighten a whole room. The light from the spotlights below does not travel in all directions. The sides of the spotlight direct the light to travel in one direction. Light can pass through some of the objects it strikes. For example, light can pass through a window or a glass of water. These objects do not block all light that passes through them.

1. **List** Write three objects that do not block all light.

How Light Changes

The path of light can change in different ways. Light can be reflected, refracted, or absorbed.

Reflect

You can see an object because light **reflects,** or bounces off the object. Some objects reflect light better than others. Flat, smooth surfaces reflect light evenly. A mirror or a smooth lake reflects light evenly. Other objects do not reflect light evenly. A rough lake does not reflect light evenly.

Refract

What happens to light in an ice cube? The ice cube **refracts,** or bends, light. Refracted light changes direction. The ice cube below refracts light that reflects off the strawberry. The refracted light forms images of the strawberry.

Light refracts when it passes through different materials at different speeds. Light passing through air slows down when it enters water. This causes the straw in the glass to look broken.

2. Explain Why can you see the reflection of the insect?

refraction

3. Draw an ✗ where you see the strawberry reflected or refracted inside the ice cube.

Absorb

Have you ever wondered why you see colors? You see colors because of what happens to light when it hits different materials.

Light is made up of different colors. An object **absorbs**, or takes in, some of the light that hits it. The object reflects the rest. Most objects reflect light. Different objects absorb and reflect different colors of light. For example, red flowers reflect the color red. Red flowers absorb other colors of light. The reflected color red is what your eyes see. White light is made up of all colors of light. If an object looks white, it reflects all colors of light. If an object looks black, it absorbs all colors of light.

4. [CHALLENGE] Will you be cooler on a hot day in a light-colored shirt or a dark-colored shirt? Explain.

Light and Objects

Few materials refract light. Water and air are two materials that refract light.

5. **State** How does each water droplet change the image of the flower?

....

....

Objects such as these hot-air balloons absorb some colors of light and reflect other colors.

6. **Explain** Why do you see the color blue in a hot-air balloon?

....

....

The rocks and lake reflect light. The rocks do not have a smooth surface. They reflect light from the sky in many directions. This is why you do not see an image of the sky on the rocks.

7. **Draw** Finish drawing the reflection on the water on the next page.

refract

absorb

reflect

Shadows

On a hot summer day, you might escape the heat by standing in the shade of a tree. Did you know you are standing in a shadow?

Light travels outward from its source in all directions until it strikes an object. When light is blocked by an object, a shadow is formed. A **shadow** is a dark area made when an object blocks light between a light source and a surface. You can see shadows on surfaces. The length of the shadow depends on the angle of the light. For example, the length and direction of shadows caused by sunlight change during the day.

8. **Analyze** Why do these tables and chairs make shadows in the sunlight?

....

....

....

....

At-Home Lab

Make Shadows
Stand in a place with bright sunlight. Make a shape with your hand. Look at the shadow it makes. Make the shadow look sharper. Make the shadow look fuzzier.

myscienceonLine.com | Got *it?* 60-Second Video

7:00 A.M.

The morning shadow of the bicycle is long. The morning shadow stretches west when the sun is in the eastern sky.

Noon

At noon, the sun appears to have moved higher in the sky. The shadow becomes shorter.

5:00 P.M.

In the afternoon, the sun appears to have moved across the sky. The shadow becomes longer. The afternoon shadow stretches east when the sun is in the western sky.

9. Describe Tell how the length and direction of the bicycle shadows above change during the day.

Got it?

3.1.4, 3.1.5, 3.1.6, 3.NS.1

10. Contrast How are reflection and refraction different?

....

....

11. Demonstrate How might you demonstrate that light can travel in a straight line?

....

....

....

⬛ **Stop!** I need help with ....

⏸ **Wait!** I have a question about ....

▶ **Go!** Now I know ....

How does sound energy move?

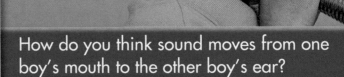

3.1.3 Investigate and recognize that sound moves through solids, liquids and gases (air). (Also 3.1.6, 3.NS.4)

How do you think sound moves from one boy's mouth to the other boy's ear?

my planet Diary

Sound waves are bouncing around inside the seashell.

//// MISCONCEPTION ////

Have you ever held a seashell to your ear? You can usually hear a sound like the sounds made by moving water or wind. Did someone tell you it was the sound of the ocean or even blood moving inside your body? The sound you hear is neither of these things. It is a mixture of many sounds around you!

There are sounds all around you. The sounds are moving at different speeds and in different directions. A seashell can trap some sounds that are all around you. When you hold a seashell to your ear, many of the sounds inside bounce into your ear. This allows you to listen closely to the sounds. Together, the sounds are like those made by water or wind.

List Write two objects you think can trap sound waves like a seashell. Explain.

....

....

I will know how sound moves through solids, liquids, and gases.

Word to Know

vibration

Sound Around You

There are sounds all around you. If you walked along a busy street, you might hear noises made by people, dogs, or machines. What do you think you would hear if those same people, dogs, and machines were on the moon? You would hear nothing!

Sound energy only moves through matter. Matter is anything that takes up space and has mass. Air is matter. There is no matter like air for sound to move through on the moon. Matter is all around us on Earth. That is why you hear so many sounds. It is also why sounds can move a long distance.

1. **Apply** Why would someone be able to hear the sounds a computer makes?

....

....

....

How Sound Moves

When you hit a drum with a drumstick, it makes sound. But how does the sound move through the air from the drum to your ear? All sounds travel in waves. These waves form when matter vibrates. A **vibration** is a quick back-and-forth movement. Vibrations in matter cause the particles that make up air to vibrate, too.

Think about the sound of the drum. As the drum vibrates, it causes the air particles around it to move. A particle is a tiny piece of matter. The moving particles form waves. In some parts of the sound wave, the air particles are squeezed together. In other parts, the particles spread apart. This pattern repeats as the drum continues to vibrate.

As a sound wave travels, the air particles that make up the wave do not move along with it. They vibrate in place and bump into each other. When they bump, energy transfers from one particle to the next. In this way, the sound energy moves through the air from particle to particle until it reaches your ear.

3. Identify (Circle) the areas in the diagram where air particles are squeezed together.

2. **CHALLENGE** Suppose you build a chain of dominoes and knock over the first one. As each domino falls, it knocks over the one next to it. In what way is this a good model for the way sound energy moves through air?

....

....

....

Sound waves move outward from the drum, the source of the sound. The diagram shows the organization of air particles in a sound wave.

At-Home Lab

Sounds Like Metal
Tie a string to each side of a metal coat hanger. Tie a loop at the end of each string. Place each loop around a finger on each hand. Place a finger in each ear. Move to make the hanger hit a table. Tell how the sound moves to your ears.

Sound and Matter

Sound travels through matter. The matter can be a solid, liquid, or gas. Sound moves through different kinds of matter at different speeds. Temperature and other factors can affect the speed of a sound traveling through matter.

Sound and Solids

Sound usually moves more quickly through closely packed particles than through particles that are spread out. Solids are made up of many closely packed particles. Sound moves quickly through solids.

Sound and Liquids

In general, sounds move more slowly through liquids than solids. In most liquids, the particles are farther apart than the particles in solids. So it takes more time for the particles in liquids to bump into each other.

The sound made by an elephant's footstep moves through the ground. Some animals can hear this sound from miles away.

4. **Explain** When sea lions communicate underwater, sound moves through liquids. How does the sound move through water?

....

....

....

....

....

Sound and Gases

Air is made of gas. The particles in gases are farther apart than in solids and liquids. So for most gases, it takes longer for one gas particle to hit another and move the sound energy along.

5. **Solve** These penguins are moving sound through air, a gas. If sound travels 340 meters per second in the air, how far away is the source of a sound that takes two seconds to reach your ear?

Got it?　　🔘 3.1.3, 3.1.6, 3.NS.4

6. **Recognize** How does sound energy move through solids, liquids, and gases?

....

....

7. 🔘 **Cause and Effect** When a car honks its horn, what happens to the matter around it?

....

....

....

⬛ **Stop!** I need help with ....

⏸ **Wait!** I have a question about ....

▶ **Go!** Now I know ....

What are volume and pitch?

Envision It!

3.1.1 Generate sounds using different materials, objects and techniques; record; discuss and share results. 3.1.2 Investigate how the loudness and pitch of sound changes when the rate of vibrations changes. (Also 3.1.6, 3.NS.1, 3.NS.3)

Write words to describe the sound you think this party blower makes.

Inquiry **Explore It!**

What can affect the sound made by a rubber band?

☐ **1.** Stretch a thick rubber band and a thin rubber band around a box.

☐ **2. Observe** Pluck each band. How does each sound? **Record.**

....

....

☐ **3.** Slide a ruler under the bands. Turn the edge up. Pluck each band. How does each band sound?

....

Explain Your Results

4. Draw a Conclusion How does a rubber band's thickness affect its sound?

....

....

Materials

safety goggles

thick rubber band

thin rubber band

plastic tub (or shoebox)

ruler

Be careful! **Wear safety goggles. Be careful not to snap the rubber bands.**

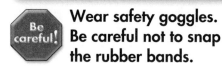

myscienceonline.com | **Explore It!** Animation

3.NS.8 Identify simple patterns in data and propose explanations to account for the patterns. (Also 3.1.3)

I will know how different vibrations make different sounds.

Words to Know

volume

pitch

Different Sounds

At a party, you might hear loud music and noisemakers. In a field, you might hear crickets chirp quietly. On the sidewalk, you might hear car horns. You hear many different sounds every day. Sound happens when matter vibrates.

Each sound has certain characteristics. Some sounds are loud, and others are soft. You may enjoy the sound of loud music. Yet the sound of an airplane taking off may hurt your ears. You can hear high sounds and low sounds. Some sounds are so high that only some animals can hear them.

1. ◉ **Cause and Effect** Complete the graphic organizer to show an effect.

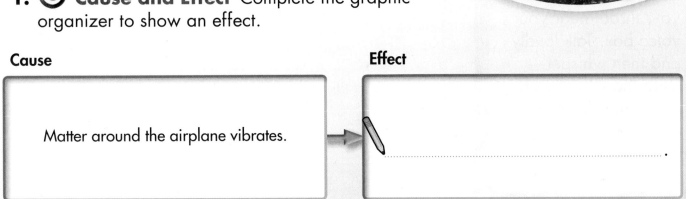

Cause	Effect
Matter around the airplane vibrates.	....

A siren sounds very loud if you are standing near it.

Volume

Sound waves can have different properties. Because of this, the sounds we hear have different properties. Think about the siren on a fire truck. The first thing you might notice about a siren is its **volume,** or how loud or soft a sound is. Volume is a property of sound. Volume is related to how much energy a sound has.

When you whisper, you make a soft sound. The sound waves you create have little energy. When you shout, you use more energy to make a sound. The sound waves you create have more energy. The sound is louder.

Volume also depends on how far away a listener is from the source of the sound. Suppose you are near a siren when it goes off. The sound would not have to travel far to get to your ears. But if you are far away, the siren would not seem as loud. The sound waves do not lose energy as they travel away from the siren. But the energy spreads out in all directions over a larger area.

2. **Illustrate** Draw a picture to show how sound spreads out as it moves away from a roaring lion.

Lightning Lab

Change Vibrations, Change Sounds

Rest your fingers on your throat near your voice box. Talk loudly and then whisper. Describe what you feel each time. Tell what changes when you make softer or louder sounds.

Sporting events can be very loud. The cheers of each person in the crowd produce sound waves and carry energy. Together, the cheers have a very loud volume.

3. ⊙ **Cause and Effect** What might cause the volume of the crowd to be even louder?

....

....

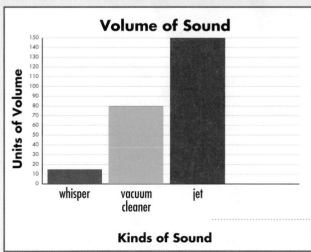

Read a Graph

Use the graph to compare pairs of sounds. For each item below, fill in the blank with **louder** or **softer**. Then complete the number sentence by writing in the correct symbol (**>** or **<**).

1 A vacuum cleaner is

.... than a

jet. **80**   **150**

2 A vacuum cleaner is

.... than a

whisper. **80**   **15**

3 A chain saw produces 100 units of volume. Draw and label a bar for chain saw on the bar graph.

The bar graph shows the loudness of some sounds measured in units of volume.

Volume of Sound

Units of Volume

150
140
130
120
110
100
90
80
70
60
50
40
30
20
10
0

whisper   vacuum   jet
           cleaner

Kinds of Sound

This songbird can make sounds of many different pitches. Its voice sounds musical.

Pitch

How is the song of a bird different from the roar of a lion? It certainly is softer than the lion's roar. It is different in another way too.

A bird makes a higher sound than a lion. **Pitch** is how high or low a sound is. The bird makes a high-pitched sound. The lion makes a low-pitched sound.

A sound's pitch depends on its frequency. The frequency of a sound is the number of sound waves made in a certain amount of time. Objects that vibrate quickly have a high frequency. High-frequency sounds have a high pitch. Objects that vibrate slowly have a low frequency and a low pitch.

The material an object is made of affects its pitch. The size and shape of an object also affect pitch. For example, a small drum will usually have a higher pitch than a big drum.

4. ◎ **Compare and Contrast** A songbird and a lion make different sounds. Use the words *high* and *low* to compare their pitch.

....

....

....

5. **Apply** The wooden blocks at left make sound when hit with a rubber hammer. **Circle** the block that you think has the highest pitch. Explain.

....

....

Pitch in Stringed Instruments

Guitars, violins, cellos, and harps are kinds of stringed instruments. Stringed instruments make sound when you pluck their strings or rub a bow across their strings. Each string's pitch depends on the string's properties. A thin string vibrates faster than a thick string, so a thin string has higher pitch. In the same way, a short or tight string vibrates faster than a long or loose string. So the string that is shorter or tighter makes a sound with a higher pitch.

6. **Infer** If the guitarist wanted the thinnest string on the guitar to produce an even higher pitch, what could the guitarist do?

Each string of a guitar has a different pitch.

Got it?

🅘 3.1.1, 3.1.2, 3.1.6, 3.NS.1, 3.NS.3

7. ◎ **Compare and Contrast** Use the words *loud* and *soft* to compare the sounds of a bicycle and a large truck.

8. **Predict** A guitar has thick strings and thin strings. Would you expect the thick strings to sound higher or lower than the thin strings? Explain why.

⬛ **Stop!** I need help with ....

⏸ **Wait!** I have a question about ....

▶ **Go!** Now I know ....

What makes sound change?

Follow a Procedure

☐ **1.** Tie one end of a string around the neck of a bottle. Tie the other end to a marker.

☐ **2.** Use a funnel. Fill the bottle about $\frac{1}{3}$ full with water. Screw the cap tightly onto bottle.

☐ **3.** Hang the bottle from the string.

Materials

pitcher of water   plastic 2 L bottle with cap

funnel

marker   string

Pluck the string here.

Hold the marker on the table.

Almost touching the floor.

Inquiry Skill
Use your observations to **infer** why something happens.

☐ **4. Observe**   What happens when you pluck the string?

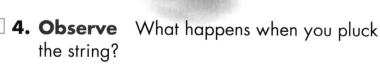

3.1.2 Investigate how the loudness and pitch of sound changes when the rate of vibrations changes. **3.NS.7** Keep accurate records in a notebook during investigations and communicate findings to others using graphs, charts, maps and models through oral and written reports. **3.NS.9** Compare the results of an investigation with the prediction. (Also **3.1.1**, **3.NS.8**)

5. Use the chart below to make changes. How does the sound change? First, make a prediction. Then, conduct multiple trials. **Record** your observation.

Pitch Chart		
Change	**Predictions**	**Observations**
Add water to the bottle.		
Pluck the string gently and then pluck it hard.		
Shorten the string.		

Analyze and Conclude

6. Predict What will happen to the sound if you take most of the water out of the bottle? Test your prediction. Use multiple trials.

....

7. Infer Look for a pattern. How does the length of the string affect the pitch? Propose an explanation.

....

....

....

8. UNLOCK THE BIG **Observe** How did the energy change when you plucked the string gently and then hard?

....

....

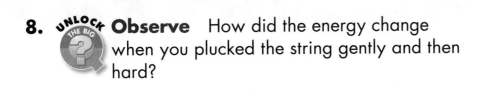

Recording Studio

Recording studios have been around since the late 1800s. They are found all across the United States. Music for movies, television shows, and the radio are recorded in recording studios. People use recording studios to record songs, commercials, and anything with sound.

A recording studio is usually made up of two rooms. The first room is called the studio. This is where people sing, play instruments, or talk. It is very important that outside noises do not interrupt the sounds in the studio.

The other room is called the control room. This is where the sound is recorded. The equipment in the control room is used for recording and managing the sounds coming from the studio. A microphone is used to send sound waves from the studio to the control room. Another piece of equipment is the soundboard. It helps adjust the sounds coming from the recording studio. A multitrack recorder allows sounds to be recorded at separate times and put together later.

Recording studios allow sounds to be saved and played as often as people like.

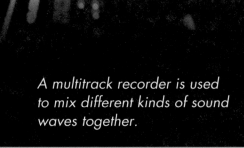

A multitrack recorder is used to mix different kinds of sound waves together.

APPLY THE BIG ?

How does energy change in a recording studio?

....

....

....

Vocabulary Smart Cards

energy
electrical energy
mechanical energy
sound energy
potential energy
kinetic energy
wave
light energy
reflect
refract
absorb
shadow
vibration
volume
pitch

Play a Game!

Choose a Vocabulary Smart Card.

Write a sentence using the vocabulary word. Draw a blank where the vocabulary word should be.

Have a partner fill in the blank with the correct vocabulary word.

Have your partner repeat with another card.

157

sound energy

energía sonora

energy

energía

potential energy

energía potencial

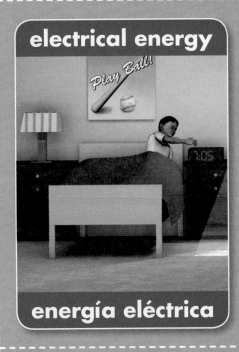

electrical energy

energía eléctrica

kinetic energy

energía cinética

mechanical energy

energía mecánica

the ability to do work or to cause change

Write three other forms of this word.

....

....

....

capacidad de hacer trabajo o causar cambios

---

energy we can hear

Draw an example.

energía que podemos oír

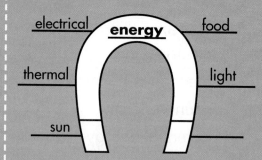

electrical — energy — food

thermal — light

sun —

Make a Word Magnet!

Choose a vocabulary word and write it in the Word Magnet. Write words that are related to it on the lines.

---

the movement of electric charges

Draw an example.

el movimiento de cargas eléctricas

---

stored energy

Write two examples.

....

....

....

....

energía almacenada

---

energy that motion or position gives to an object

Write a sentence using this term.

....

....

....

energía que un objeto obtiene por su posición o desplazamiento

---

energy of motion

Write a sentence using this term.

....

....

....

energía de movimiento

vibration

vibración

refract

refractar

wave

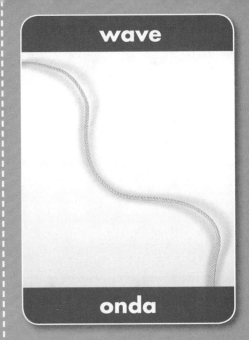

onda

volume

volumen

absorb

absorber

light energy

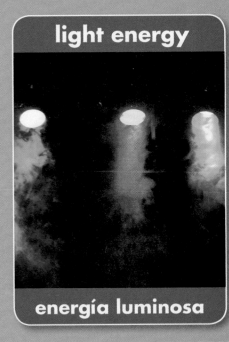

energía luminosa

pitch

tono

shadow

sombra

reflect

reflejar

a disturbance that carries energy from one point to another point

Write another meaning of this word.

....

....

....

perturbación que lleva energía de un punto a otro

to bend

Write three other forms of this word.

....

....

....

....

desviar o inclinar

a quick back-and-forth movement

Write a synonym for this word.

....

....

....

movimiento rápido hacia delante y hacia atrás

energy we can see

Write two examples.

....

....

....

....

....

energía que podemos ver

to take in

Write a sentence using this word.

....

....

....

....

....

retener

how loud or soft a sound is

Write a sentence using this word.

....

....

....

....

cuán fuerte o suave es un sonido

to bounce off

Write a sentence using the noun form of this word.

....

....

....

....

hacer rebotar algo

a dark area made when an object blocks light between a light source and a surface

Draw an example.

región oscura que se produce cuando un objeto colocado entre una fuente de luz y una superficie bloquea la luz

how high or low a sound is

Write an example of a sound with a high pitch.

....

....

....

....

cuán agudo o grave es un sonido

What is energy?

- Energy is the ability to do work and cause change.
- Energy makes things move, change, or grow.
- People use many forms of energy every day.

Lesson 2

What are some ways energy changes form?

- Energy can change from one form to another.
- Energy of motion can be transferred.
- Some energy travels as waves.

Lesson 3

How do light and matter interact?

- Objects can reflect light evenly or unevenly.
- Some objects refract light.
- Some objects absorb some of the colors of light that hit them.

Lesson 4

How does sound energy move?

- Sound happens when matter vibrates.
- Sounds move through solids, liquids, and gases at different speeds.

Lesson 5

What are volume and pitch?

- A sound's pitch is how high or low the sound is.
- A sound's energy determines how loud or soft the volume is.

Chapter Review

REVIEW THE BIG ?

How can energy change?

Lesson 1 — 3.1.1, 3.1.3, 3.1.6, 3.NS.3

What is energy?

1. Determine (Circle) the image that shows kinetic energy.

2. Analyze What is one way that stored energy can change to become energy of motion?

Lesson 2 — 3.1.3, 3.NS.1

What are some ways energy changes form?

Do the math!

3. Solve Marcus ran a 100-meter race at a speed of 5 meters per second. How long did it take him to finish the race?

Rule: Time = Distance ÷ Speed

---

4. ⊙ Cause and Effect When you turn on an electric toothbrush, chemical energy in the battery changes to electrical energy. In the graphic organizer below, list two additional energy changes that happen as a result.

Cause

| Chemical energy changes to electrical energy. |

Effect

Effect

Lesson 3 • 3.1.4, 3.1.5, 3.1.6, 3.NS.1

How do light and matter interact?

5. Infer Light reflecting off an object scatters in many directions. What can you infer about the object?

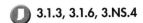

6. Vocabulary A blue book _____ blue light that strikes it.
A. colors
B. absorbs
C. reflects
D. shadows

Lesson 4 • 3.1.3, 3.1.6, 3.NS.4

How does sound energy move?

7. Explain What is different about how sound moves through solids, liquids, and gases?

Lesson 5 • 3.1.1, 3.1.2, 3.1.6, 3.NS.1, 3.NS.3

What are volume and pitch?

8. Predict A bell vibrates quickly when you ring it. Will the bell have a high pitch or a low pitch? Explain.

9. APPLY THE BIG **How can energy change?**

Think about a trip to the grocery store. What was one form of energy being used? Explain how this energy can change form.

Multiple Choice

1 Which word describes the pitch of a guitar string vibrating slowly?

A. loud

B. low

C. high

D. soft

 3.1.2

Constructed Response

2 Light energy allows people to see colors. Explain why people see the color yellow when they look at a banana.

....

....

....

....

....

....

 3.1.5

Extended Response

3 Sounds can move through solids, liquids, and gases. Maggie investigated how quickly sound traveled through each type of matter. Her results are shown in the table below.

Speed of Sound

Material	Speed (meters per second)
Solid—Steel	5,200
Liquid—Seawater	1,530
Gas—Air	340

Did sound travel faster through seawater or steel?

....

....

Why do you think sound traveled slowest through air?

....

....

What is another solid material Maggie could have used in her investigation?

....

....

 3.1.3

myscienceonline.com | ISTEP+ Practice

Electrical Energy Conservation

We use electrical energy every day. We use electrical energy to light our homes and run appliances, such as televisions and refrigerators. Most electrical energy comes from nonrenewable sources. After a nonrenewable source of energy is used, it cannot be replaced. Most electricity in the United States is made from the burning of coal. Coal is a nonrenewable source of energy.

Scientists are developing different sources of energy to use instead of nonrenewable sources. For example, scientists are working to develop solar energy and wind energy. Meanwhile, we can reduce the amount of energy we use by following the tips on this page.

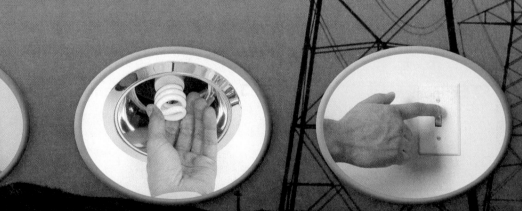

Use a thermostat with a timer.

Use compact fluorescent light bulbs.

Turn off lights when leaving a room.

Suggest Write two more ways you can conserve electrical energy in your home.

Materials

3 cups

masking tape

marker

water

graduated cylinder

table salt

plastic spoon

3 thermometers

tub of ice

timer or stopwatch

How does salt affect the way water cools?

Ask a question.

Does salt affect how water cools?

State a hypothesis.

1. Write a **hypothesis** by circling one choice and finishing the sentence. If salt is added to water, it will cool

(a) *the same as*

(b) *faster than*

(c) *slower than*

pure tap water because

....

....

Identify and control variables.

2. In an **experiment** you change only one **variable.** Everything else must remain the same. What must stay the same? Give one example.

....

....

....

3. Tell the one change you will make.

....

....

....

Inquiry Skill

You **experiment** when you design a way to answer a scientific question.

3.4.1 Choose and use the appropriate tools to estimate measure length, mass and temperature in SI units. **3.NS.1** Make predictions and formulate testable questions. **3.NS.2** Design a fair test. **3.NS.5** Use measurement skills and apply appropriate units when collecting data. (Also **3.NS.7**, **3.NS.9**)

Design your test.

☑ **4.** Draw how you will set up your test.

☑ **5.** List your steps in the order you will do them.

Do your test.

☑ **6.** Follow the steps you wrote.

☑ **7. Measure** accurately. **Record** your results in the table.

Collect and record your data.

☑ **8.** Fill in the chart.

Interpret your data.

☑ **9.** Heat moved from the liquid in the cups to the ice. Compare how the temperature in the different cups changed.

....

....

....

....

☐ **10.** Did adding salt cause the water to cool faster?

....

....

State your conclusion.

11. Communicate How did adding salt affect how water cools? Compare your **hypothesis** with your results. Compare your results with other students.

....

....

....

....

....

Work Like a Scientist
Scientists compare their methods and results with other scientists. Communicate with your classmates. Compare your methods and results with other students.

Make an Instrument

Make your own musical instrument. Your instrument should be able to make sounds of different volumes and pitches. You might make an instrument similar to guitar or a flute. You may use shoe boxes, rubber bands, cans, bottles, straws, or other items. Give a demonstration to your class about how your instrument makes sounds of different volumes and pitches.

3.1.2

Toy Power

Choose a wind-up toy. Observe the toy as it works. Look for ways the toy transfers energy from one part to another.

• How does you wind up the toy affect the distance it travels?

• How might some kinetic energy be transferred from one part to another?

3.NS.3

Write a Poem

Write a poem about matter. Include at least four properties of matter. You may want to select some objects and describe them in your poem. Here are some tips to help you write your poem.

• A poem is written in lines.

• A poem may rhyme or have a rhythm.

3.1.3

Using Scientific Methods

1. Ask a question.

2. State your hypothesis.

3. Identify and control variables.

4. Test your hypothesis.

5. Collect and record your data.

6. Interpret your data.

7. State your conclusion.

8. Go further.

Earth
Science

How can a **tree** break apart a mountain?

Minerals and Rocks

 Try It! How are minerals alike and different?

Investigate It! What are the properties of minerals?

Trees and mountains seem to never change. Yet Earth's resources are always changing, and living things interact with them. Earth's resources help shape what Earth's surface looks like.

 Predict How could a tree break apart rock?

....

....

....

THE BIG ? How do Earth's resources change?

How are minerals alike and different?

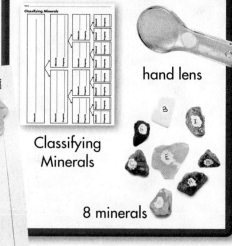

Materials

hand lens

Classifying Minerals

8 minerals

☑ **1. Observe** the minerals with a hand lens.

☑ **2.** Place all the minerals in the top rectangle on the Classifying Minerals sheet.

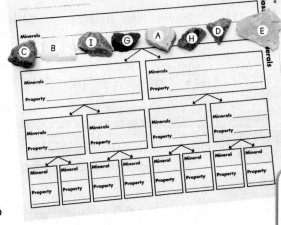

☑ **3. Classify** Divide the minerals into 2 equal groups. List the property used to sort the minerals.

Inquiry Skill
Observing minerals carefully can help you **classify** them.

☑ **4.** Divide each group equally into 2 groups again.

☑ **5.** Finally, divide the groups so each mineral is in a separate box.

Explain Your Results

6. **UNLOCK THE BIG ?** **Classify** Think about the properties you used to classify each mineral. In the chart below, identify those properties.

How Are Minerals Alike and Different?			
A	**B**	**C**	**D**
E	**G**	**H**	**I**

3.2.1 Examine the physical properties of rock samples and sort them into categories based on size using simple tools such as sieves. **3.2.2** Observe the detailed characteristics of rocks and minerals and identify rocks as being composed of different combinations of minerals. (Also **3.2.3**, **3.NS.4**)

◉ Compare and Contrast

- When you **compare** things, you tell how they are alike.
- When you **contrast** things, you tell how they are different.

Two Forms of Quartz

An amethyst is the purple form of the mineral quartz. Citrines are quartz, too, but they are yellow or orange. Both amethysts and citrines are used in rings, necklaces, and other jewelry. However, citrines are usually less expensive than amethysts.

Practice It!

Complete the graphic organizer to show how amethysts and citrines are alike and different.

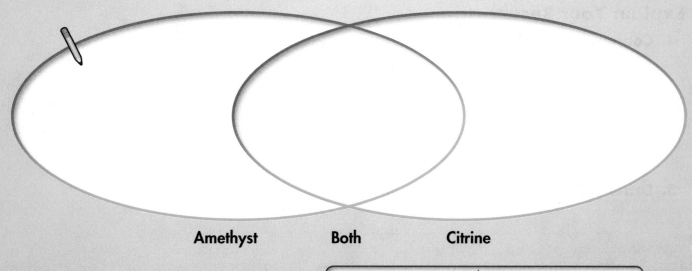

Amethyst   Both   Citrine

What are minerals?

3.2.2 Observe the detailed characteristics of rocks and minerals and identify rocks as being composed of different combinations of minerals. 3.2.3 Observe, classify, and identify minerals by their physical properties of hardness, color, luster, and streak. (Also 3.2.5, 3.2.6, 3.NS.4, 3.NS.8)

Tell where you think there are minerals at this quarry.

Inquiry ▸ Explore It!

What do mineral crystals look like?

☐ **1.** Place a few crystals of Mineral A on a slide. **Observe.**

☐ **2.** Repeat Step 1 using Mineral B.

☐ **3.** Compare these pictures with the minerals.

salt

alum

Materials

mineral A   mineral B

2 microscope slides

microscope   2 toothpicks

Be careful! Wash your hands after handling the minerals.

Explain Your Results

4. Communicate Compare and contrast the crystals.

....

....

....

5. Draw a Conclusion Identify the minerals.

....

myscienceonline.com | ◄ **Explore It!** Animation

3.NS.4 Perform investigations using appropriate tools and technology that will extend the senses. (Also **3.NS.3**)

I will know how to classify and identify minerals by their hardness, color, luster, and streak.

Words to Know

mineral   streak
luster

Minerals

Minerals are the most common solid material on Earth. A **mineral** is a natural, nonliving material that makes up rocks. Minerals are composed of chemicals.

Some common minerals can be found in many locations on Earth. Rock salt and quartz are common minerals. Other minerals are rare, or hard to find. For example, gold and silver are rare minerals. Minerals come in many different shapes. They also have different colors and textures.

These stalactites in Marengo Cave in Indiana are made from minerals.

1. ◉ **Compare and Contrast** Complete the graphic organizer to show how common minerals and rare minerals are alike and different.

Common minerals   Both   Rare minerals

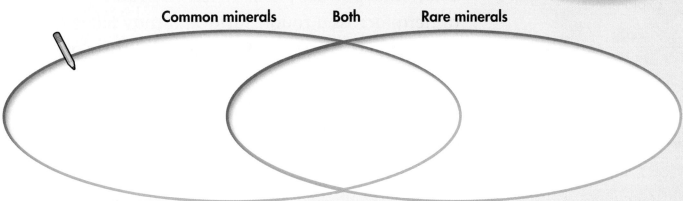

Lightning Lab

Identify a Mineral

Select a mineral you do not know. Record its color and luster. Rub the mineral on a rough surface. Record its streak. Then record its hardness. Research these properties to identify the mineral.

2. **Analyze** Which property would you use to identify a mineral? Explain.

....

....

....

....

Identifying Minerals

Minerals have physical properties such as texture. They have other properties, too. A property is something that you can observe with one or more of your senses. Scientists identify minerals by their properties.

Hardness

One way to identify a mineral is to test its hardness. For example, the mineral talc is soft enough to scratch with your fingernail. The hardest mineral is a diamond. It can be scratched only by another diamond.

Color

Color is a property you notice easily about a mineral. But some minerals can be found in different colors. For example, the mineral quartz can be pink, purple, yellow, brown, white, or black.

Luster

Minerals are also identified by their luster. **Luster** is the way a mineral reflects light. Minerals can be metallic, glassy, pearly, silky, greasy, or dull.

Streak

Another way to identify a mineral is by the color of its powder form. When you rub a mineral across a rough surface, it may leave a streak mark or powder. **Streak** is the color of the powder that a mineral leaves when it is rubbed across a rough surface. The streak of a mineral is always the same color, even if pieces of the mineral are different colors.

Properties of Minerals

Mineral	Hardness	Color	Luster	Streak
Halite	can be scratched with a penny	white, clear, pink, blue	glassy	white
Copper	can be scratched with a knife blade	reddish brown	metallic	reddish brown
Fluorite	can be scratched with a knife blade	white, purple, blue, red	glassy	
Pyrite	can be scratched with a steel file	gold, yellow	metallic	

3. Identify Circle the minerals that have a glassy luster and white streak.

4. Observe Look at the streaks of fluorite and pyrite in the chart. Write the colors of the streaks.

Minerals in Objects

5. Apply How have you used minerals today?

....

....

Many things we use are made from or contain minerals. For example, the graphite in your pencil is a mineral. Most cans that you drink from are made from the mineral aluminum. Quartz is used to make products such as glass, computers, and radios.

Minerals in Our Bodies

Minerals are important to our bodies. People need minerals to keep their bodies healthy. For example, the mineral iron is found in red meats, beans, and leafy green vegetables. Iron is important because your blood to uses it to carry oxygen. The mineral calcium helps keep our bones and teeth strong. The mineral sodium helps control water levels. Sodium also helps carry messages through nerves.

Do the math!

Add and Multiply

Iron is an important mineral. It helps your body grow. Foods such as whole wheat, red meat, and dried fruit are good sources of iron. It is healthy to eat 10 mg of iron per day.

The chart below shows how much iron a student ate in one day.

Food	Iron
Black Beans	4 mg
Hamburger	3 mg
Raisins	2 mg

1 Did the student eat enough iron for the day?

....

2 Solve If not, how much more would the student need to eat?

....

3 Solve If the student ate 10 mg of iron every day for 5 days, how much iron would the student have eaten?

....

myscienceonline.com | Got *it?* 60-Second Video

Minerals Everywhere

Minerals are found everywhere, including in your home. Minerals are found in both objects and food.

6. Observe Look at the image. Write two objects you see and the minerals in them.

....

....

Got it?

3.2.2, 3.2.3, 3.2.5, 3.2.6, 3.NS.4, 3.NS.8

7. State What are four properties of a mineral you can observe to identify it?

....

....

8. Identify Write about the hardness, color, luster, and streak of a mineral.

....

....

Stop! I need help with ....

Wait! I have a question about ....

Go! Now I know ....

What are rocks?

3.2.2 Observe the detailed characteristics of rocks and minerals and identify rocks as being composed of different combinations of minerals. **3.2.6** Describe how the properties of earth materials make them useful to humans in different ways and describe ways that humans have altered these resources to meet their needs for survival. (Also **3.NS.1, 3.NS.7, 3.NS.8**)

Envision It!

Circle the two rocks that you think are the same. Explain.

my planet DiaRY

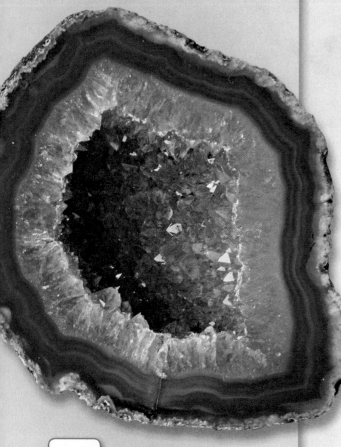

agate

FunFact

Agate is a unique stone. It is known for its beautiful colors. However, those colors are often different. You can find agate in colors such as pink, red, purple, blue, and green. The color of each agate stone is affected by factors such as temperature, weathering, and the minerals in the stone. It can be one solid color, polka dotted, or striped.

Agate is usually formed in volcanoes. It is formed from layers of quartz. Agate can be found in many states and countries. It is the state stone of Kentucky, Louisiana, and Nebraska.

Interpret Why do you think agate is found in so many places?

....

....

....

I will know what rocks are made from. I will know how rocks are grouped.

Words to Know

rock
igneous rock
sedimentary rock
metamorphic rock

Rocks

Rocks are everywhere on Earth. **Rock** is natural, solid, nonliving material made of one mineral or a combination of minerals. You can tell rocks apart by looking at their physical properties.

The physical properties of rocks include color, what minerals they are made of, and texture. Texture is the size and shape of the bits of minerals, or grains, that make up rock. Some rocks may have grains that are big enough to see. These different sizes of minerals make rocks feel smooth, rough, or bumpy.

1. **Describe** Look at the pictures to the right. How does granite resemble quartz and feldspar?

....

....

....

Quartz and feldspar are minerals that make up granite rock.

Types of Rocks

There are different types of rocks. Rocks can differ in texture, color, and how heavy they feel. They can also share some similar characteristics. Rocks can be placed into three main groups. Rocks in each group are formed in a certain way. Each group contains many kinds of rocks.

Igneous Rock

Small amounts of melted rock sometimes form beneath Earth's surface. **Igneous rock** forms when melted rock cools and hardens. The word igneous means "from fire." Sometimes the melted rock cools slowly below ground. Then the mineral grains in the igneous rock may be large. Other times the melted rock comes to the surface and cools quickly. Then the grains may be too small to see. Igneous rocks are usually made of two or more minerals. They have different colors ranging from light to dark.

2. **Infer** This igneous rock is called obsidian. Did it form above ground or below? How do you know?

....

....

....

Igneous rock can come from volcanoes.

Sedimentary Rock

Rock that forms from sediments is called **sedimentary rock.** Sediments are tiny bits of rock, sand, shells, and other materials. Sediments settle to the bottom of rivers, lakes, and oceans. Over millions of years, the sediments are pressed together and cemented to form sedimentary rock. Sedimentary rock forms in layers—one layer at a time. Sedimentary rock usually has a flat shape. Sedimentary rocks are found in a variety of colors. They may have cracks from mud or dents from raindrops.

This canyon wall is made of sandstone, a sedimentary rock.

3. Distinguish Circle the oldest layer of the canyon wall you can see.

Rock Detective

Gather ten rocks. Observe their colors, textures, and shapes. Which rock group do you think each belongs to—igneous, sedimentary, or metamorphic? Record your observations in a chart.

4. **Recall** What two forces cause shale to change into slate?

Metamorphic Rock

Metamorphic means "that changes form." Rock that has been changed by heat and pressure is called **metamorphic rock.** Shale is a sedimentary rock. Heat and pressure underground change the minerals in the shale. The shale becomes slate, a metamorphic rock. Granite is an igneous rock. It can be changed into gneiss, a metamorphic rock. Metamorphic rocks can have alternate strips of light and dark minerals. Some metamorphic rocks, such as marble, are composed of only one mineral.

5. CHALLENGE A metamorphic rock can be changed into sedimentary rock. Explain how this might happen.

....

....

....

Look at the chart below.
It shows how rocks can change from one type to another.

Igneous	Sedimentary
Granite Granite is igneous rock that has large grains. Granite is often used in building materials.	**Shale** Shale is a sedimentary rock with thin layers.
Changed into	
Metamorphic	
Gneiss This gneiss was once granite. The grains in gneiss are arranged in layers.	**Slate** This slate was once shale. Slate also has thin layers.

Uses of Rocks

Rocks are used for their beauty, strength, and function. People use rocks to make buildings and tools. Limestone is used in construction. Shale and granite are used to make bricks. Chalkboards and roofing shingles are made out of slate. Cars and bicycles move on roads that are made of asphalt. Asphalt is made from crushed rock and is usually black in color.

6. **Determine** How were rocks used to build this building?

....

....

Wabash College in Crawfordsville, Indiana

Got it? 🟦 **3.2.2, 3.2.6, 3.NS.1, 3.NS.7, 3.NS.8**

7. **Describe** What are rocks made up of?

....

....

8. **Observe** Describe metamorphic rocks using two characteristics.

....

....

⏹ **Stop!** I need help with ....

⏸ **Wait!** I have a question about ....

▶ **Go!** Now I know ....

How do you sort rocks?

Envision It!

3.2.1 Examine the physical properties of rock samples and sort them into categories based on size using simple tools such as sieves. 3.NS.5 Use measurement skills and apply appropriate units when collecting data. (Also 3.NS.1)

Tell what kind of rocks you see in the Indiana Sand Dunes.

Inquiry Explore It!

How can you sort rocks?

☐ **1.** Pour the soil sample through a sieve over a paper towel. Gently shake.

☐ **2.** Remove the rocks from the sieve. Sort them.

☐ **3.** Pour the sand and silt in a jar with water.

☐ **4.** Put the lid on the jar and shake for 15 seconds. Set this aside for 5 minutes. **Observe.**

 Be careful! Wash your hands after handling the rocks.

Explain Your Results

5. What did you **observe** in the jar?

....

....

....

6. Classify What property did you use to sort the rocks?

....

....

Materials

mixture of small rocks, pebbles, sand, and silt

sieve

jar with lid and water

paper towels

clock with second hand

myscienceonline.com | **Explore It!** Animation

3.NS.4 Perform investigations using appropriate tools and technology that will extend the senses.

UNLOCK THE BIG ?

I will know how to sort rocks based on size. I will know how to use simple tools such as a sieve.

Words to Know

sieve   silt
boulder

Tools to Sort Rocks

Rocks can be sorted in different ways. One main way is to sort rocks by size. You can use a sieve to sort rocks by their sizes. A **sieve** is a tool used for separating materials. Sieves help separate larger materials from smaller materials. For example, a sieve can separate a rock from a pile of sand. Different sieves have different sized holes.

Other tools also allow people to sort rocks. A ruler can be used to measure rock size. A scale can measure rock weight.

1. ◉ **Compare and Contrast** How are the tools used to sort rocks alike and different?

....

....

....

....

2. **Conclude** Why do you think different sieves have different sized holes?

....

....

....

....

....

sieve

3. Exemplify What is another way rocks might move to different environments?

....

....

4. Solve If the person standing next to the boulder is about 2 meters tall, about how tall is the boulder?

....

Rock Size

Scientists examine the physical properties of rock samples. They use tools to sort rocks by their properties. One major property of rocks is size.

Boulders and Pebbles

Boulders and pebbles are two sizes of rock. They can share the same textures, colors, and minerals. A **boulder** is a large rock that is rounded or worn down by water and weather. Water can move boulders to different locations. This is why some boulders do not look like the other rocks around them.

A pebble is a small rock that is usually worn smooth and round by water. Pebbles are formed in rivers, lakes, and oceans.

pebbles

Boulder

Sand and Silt

Sand and silt are smaller than pebbles. Sand is found along most beaches and in deserts. Sand is tiny grains of broken rock. Sand can be different colors such as white, black, green, and yellow. **Silt** is very fine particles of earth and sand carried by moving water. A piece of silt is slightly smaller than a piece of sand. It can be found along the banks of rivers.

sand

silt

5. Contrast What are two differences between sand and silt?

....

....

....

Got it?

🕐 3.2.1, 3.NS.1, 3.NS.5

6. Rank Sort the four types of rocks in order from smallest to largest.

....

....

7. Determine Describe two tools you could use to sort rocks. Explain how you would use them.

....

....

⬛ **Stop!** I need help with ....

⏸ **Wait!** I have a question about ....

▶ **Go!** Now I know ....

What can we learn from fossils?

3.2.4 Observe fossils and describe how they provide evidence about the plants and animals that lived long ago and the nature of their environment at that time. 3.NS.8 Identify simple patterns in data and propose explanations to account for the patterns.

Tell what you think this dinosaur ate. Explain.

Inquiry Explore It!

What can a fossil tell you?

☐ **1. Make a model** of a fossil. Press a shell into clay.

☐ **2.** Work in a group. Make a fossil model with an object.

☐ **3.** Take turns making a fossil model. Guess what each fossil model shows.

Explain Your Results

4. How did you **infer** what each fossil model showed?

....

....

5. How do fossils give clues about living things?

....

....

....

....

Materials

shell

clay

objects

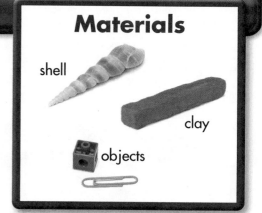

myscienceonline.com | **Explore It!** Animation

3.NS.1 Make predictions and formulate testable questions. (Also 3.NS.3)

I will know the characteristics of fossils. I will know how fossils are used to learn about the past.

Words to Know

extinct
fossil

Fossils

Many kinds of plants and animals that lived long ago are no longer living on Earth. They are **extinct.** How do scientists learn about plants and animals from the past? One way is to study fossils.

A **fossil** is the remains or mark of a living thing from long ago. Fossils are often found in sedimentary rock. The pictures show one way that fossils form. Sediments cover the remains of an animal. The sediments then turn to rock over time. As the animal's body wears away, it leaves a mold in the rock in the shape of the animal's parts.

Fossils form in other ways too. Some are actual parts of living things, such as bones. Sometimes an animal's whole body becomes a fossil. For example, scientists have found the bodies of insects in hardened tree sap. Signs of living things, such as preserved footprints, are a type of fossil too.

1. **Apply** Tell if the fossil in the bottom picture is the actual remains of a lizard. Explain how you know.

A lizard dies and is covered by mud.

The mud becomes rock. The mold of the lizard is a fossil.

2. Infer How do you think *T. rex* used its long tail?

....

....

....

....

a fern fossil

3. Predict The fern in the fossil looks black. Do you think ferns from the past were really black? Explain.

....

....

....

....

4. Identify Look at the fern and *T. rex* fossils on these pages. Tell what characteristics you see.

Tyrannosaurus rex could grow as long as a school bus.

What Fossils Show

Fossils show how plants and animals have changed over time. They also help us understand how Earth has changed.

From plant fossils, scientists have learned that many of the first plants were like today's ferns. Modern ferns live in warm, moist areas. Ferns from the past probably needed the same conditions. Scientists have found fern fossils in places that today are desert-like. The fossils are a clue that the climate in those places was once warm and wet.

Scientists also use fossils to learn how animals of the past lived. Look at the skeleton of *Tyrannosaurus rex*, a dinosaur that lived more than 65 million years ago. *T. rex* is extinct now. By studying its fossils, scientists can infer how *T. rex* lived. The sharp teeth are a sign that *T. rex* ate meat. The powerful back legs show that *T. rex* walked on two legs, not four. The thick, heavy skull? It probably protected *T. rex* from the bites of other dinosaurs.

myscienceonline.com | Got it? | 60-Second Video

lizard

5. ⊙ **Compare and Contrast** Dinosaurs were a kind of reptile. This lizard is a modern-day reptile. How are *T. rex* and the lizard alike and different?

....

....

....

Lightning Lab

Fossil Cards
Use your school's media center to find pictures of dinosaur fossils. Draw each fossil on an index card. Add notes about what the dinosaur ate and the environment it lived in. Share the cards with a partner.

Got it?

🕕 3.2.4, 3.NS.8

6. **Conclude** Scientists find the fossil of a large animal. The fossil shows that the animal had flippers and a tail. What can the scientists conclude?

....

....

7. **Explain** What can we learn about the past from studying fossil records?

....

....

⬛ **Stop!** I need help with ....

⏸ **Wait!** I have a question about ....

▶ **Go!** Now I know ....

Lesson 5

What are natural resources?

3.2.5 Describe natural materials and give examples of how they sustain the lives of plants and animals. 3.2.6 Describe how the properties of earth materials make them useful to humans in different ways and describe ways that humans have altered these resources to meet their needs for survival. (Also 3.NS.7)

Envision It!

Tell how the two pictures are related.

Inquiry **Explore It!**

How do we use natural resources?

☐ **1. Observe** each product in the *Materials* list.

☐ **2.** Match each product with its natural resource.

Natural Resources
sheep
copper ore
trees
bauxite (mined from the ground, contains aluminum)
petroleum (pumped from the ground, used to make plastic)

Materials

copper wire

paper

wool cloth

aluminum foil

plastic cup

Explain Your Results

3. Communicate Describe where each material comes from.

....

....

....

3.NS.3 Plan and carry out investigations as a class, in small groups or independently, often over a period of several class lessons.

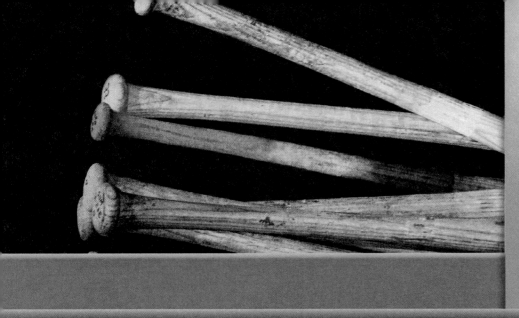

I will know how renewable and nonrenewable natural resources are used.

Words to Know

natural resource
renewable resource
nonrenewable resource

Natural Resources

The things we need come from natural resources. A **natural resource** is an important material from Earth that living things need.

Trees are a natural resource. People cut down trees for wood. Wood is used to build new houses. Wood chips are turned into pulp. Pulp is made into paper. Paper products include boxes, newspapers, and books.

Crude oil, called petroleum, is another natural resource. People use petroleum to make plastics. Plastic is in many products, including bags, bottles, and containers. There is a limited amount of petroleum on Earth.

1. **Generate** Write a list of ways trees are used at your school.

2. **State** How is this dog using water, another natural resource?

Renewable Resources

People can plant new trees to replace those cut down. If the new trees get the sunlight, air, and water they need, they can grow big enough to be cut down. A resource that can be replaced in a fairly short time is a **renewable resource.** Trees are a renewable resource. Sunlight, water, air, and soil are also renewable resources because they cannot be used up. They are all natural materials.

Sunlight

Sunlight is very important to living things. Without sunlight, many living things could not survive. Energy from the sun makes Earth's air, water, and soil warm enough for living things. Sunlight helps plants make their own food. Animals that eat plants rely on sunlight to keep plants alive.

mYscienceonLine.com | THE BIG ? | I Will Know...

Water and Air

Plants use water and air to grow. Animals need water to drink and air to breathe. Water and air are renewable resources that are always available on Earth. Yet people can use water faster than it can be renewed. People can also pollute the water and air.

Soil

Soil is another renewable resource. New soil forms as rocks break down into tiny bits. It also forms when the remains of plants and animals decay. Plants use nutrients from the soil to make food and grow. Farmers grow different plants in soil for people to eat. These plants remove valuable nutrients from the soil as they grow.

3. **Hypothesize** How might your life be different if trees were not a renewable resource?

....

....

....

....

4. **Exemplify** Look at the images. Circle the living things that use natural resources. Put an X on the renewable resources they are using.

5. **Describe** How do natural materials allow plants and animals to stay alive?

....

....

....

....

....

Petroleum is pumped from Earth by structures such as this one.

Nonrenewable Resources

A resource that cannot be replaced is a **nonrenewable resource.** Many nonrenewable resources are earth materials below the ground.

Ores

Miners dig into the ground to get rocks called ores. Ores contain metals and other minerals that people use. Copper, iron, and aluminum are some useful metals. Humans alter these resources to meet their needs. For example, copper is used to make electrical wire because it carries electricity well. The electrical wires in your home and school are likely made from copper.

Fuels

Coal, oil, and natural gas are other nonrenewable resources that come from the ground. They are fuels. When they are burned, they release useful energy. Energy from fuels can be used by humans to heat buildings or to power cars, planes, and other machines.

The supplies of ores and fuels in the ground are limited. Once we use all of these resources, they are gone forever.

6. **Describe** What properties of metals do you think make them useful to humans?

....

....

7. **Describe** How do humans alter earth materials to meet their needs for survival?

....

....

At-Home Lab

Classify Resources
List the resources you use during one day. Classify the resources as renewable or nonrenewable. Compare lists with a partner.

myscienceonline.com | Got it? 60-Second Video

Using Resources

The products we use come from natural resources. Humans alter natural resources to make many products. You can classify products according to the resources they are made from.

8. Exemplify Complete the chart. List products humans make from minerals, petroleum, and trees to meet their needs.

minerals	petroleum	trees
metal tools	plastic bags	newspapers

Got it? 〔3.2.5, 3.2.6, 3.NS.7〕

9. Explain Water is a renewable resource. How does water help keep plants and animals alive?

10. Analyze Name earth materials humans alter to make and use a car.

⬛ **Stop!** I need help with

⏸ **Wait!** I have a question about

▶ **Go!** Now I know

What are the properties of minerals?

Materials

6 minerals

streak plate   hand lens

Follow a Procedure

☐ **1.** Use a hand lens. **Observe** each mineral.

☐ **2.** **Record** their color and luster in the Table of Observed Properties on the next page.

☐ **3.** Rub each mineral across a streak plate. Record the color of its streak.

Be careful! Put the streak plate flat on the table during testing. If you hold it in your hand, it could break.

Inquiry Skill
You can use a hand lens to help you **observe.** If it has more than one power, try looking through each.

☐ **4.** Scratch Mineral A against Mineral F. Check if Mineral A is harder than Mineral F in the Table of Observed Properties.

☐ **5.** Compare the properties you observed with the Table of Diagnostic Properties. Identify each mineral.

Table of Diagnostic Properties

Mineral	Properties			
	Color	**Luster** (glassy or metallic)	**Streak**	**Hardness**
Rose quartz	pink	glassy	white	7
Calcite	white/clear	glassy	white	3
Feldspar	varied	glassy	white	6
Mica (muscovite)	varied	glassy	white	2.5
Hornblende	dark green to black	glassy	pale gray	5.5
Pyrite	gold	metallic	green to brown to black	6.5

3.2.2 Observe the detailed characteristics of rocks and minerals and identify rocks as being composed of different combinations of minerals.
3.2.3 Observe, classify, and identify minerals by their physical properties of hardness, color, luster, and streak. **3.NS.6** Test predictions with multiple trials. (Also **3.NS.4**)

202

Table of Observed Properties

Mineral	Observed Properties				Identity of Mineral
	Color	Luster (glassy or metallic)	Streak	Hardness	
Mineral A				6	
Mineral B				not measured	
Mineral C				not measured	
Mineral D				not measured	
Mineral E				not measured	
Mineral F				2.5	

Analyze and Conclude

6. What is Mineral E? Which of its properties did you **observe**?

....

....

7. What properties did you use to describe and identify the minerals?

....

....

8.  Minerals are one of Earth's important resources. What are some properties of Earth's minerals?

....

....

....

Empire State Building New York City

Big World

My World

Indiana limestone quarry

3.2.2

Indiana Limestone

Have you ever wondered where the rocks that make up your favorite tall building come from? They might be limestone from Indiana!

Indiana limestone is found in the south central region of Indiana. It is mined in eight areas across the region. In 2007, over 236,000 tons of limestone were removed from the mines.

Indiana limestone has been used to build many buildings across the United States. Buildings such as the state capitol of Indiana, the Empire State Building in New York, and the Abraham Lincoln Memorial in Washington, D.C. were constructed out of Indiana limestone. Thirty-five state capitols in the United States were also built with Indiana limestone.

Indiana limestone contains the mineral calcium carbonate. The same mineral is found in cement and makes the limestone very hard. Limestone is used in so many buildings because of its qualities and ability to resist weather damage.

APPLY THE BIG ? How have living things changed limestone on Earth's surface?

....

....

Vocabulary Smart Cards

mineral
luster
streak
rock
igneous rock
sedimentary rock
metamorphic rock
sieve
boulder
silt
extinct
fossil
natural resource
renewable resource
nonrenewable
 resource

Play a Game!

Cut out the Vocabulary Smart Cards.

Work with a partner.

Spread out two sets of Vocabulary Smart Cards on a table. One set should show the definition and the other should show the word. Pick a card and find the definition that matches the word.

Have your partner repeat with another word.

205

rock

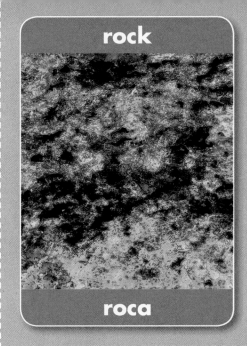

roca

mineral

mineral

igneous rock

roca ígnea

luster

brillo

sedimentary rock

roca
sedimentaria

streak

raya

natural, nonliving material that makes up rocks

Write a sentence using this word.

....

....

....

material natural y sin vida del que están formadas las rocas

natural, solid, nonliving material made from one or more minerals

What is an everyday meaning of this word?

....

....

....

material natural, sólido sin vida, compuesto por uno o más minerales

rock that forms when sediments stick together	layers of rock, sometimes with fossils
sedimentary rock	
Sandstone is a sedimentary rock.	Granite is not a sedimentary rock.

Make a Word Square!

Choose a vocabulary word and write it in the center of the square. Fill in the squares with a definition, a characteristic, an example, and something that is not an example.

the way a mineral reflects light

Write a synonym for the word luster.

....

....

manera en la que un mineral refleja la luz

rock that forms when melted rock cools and hardens

What is the suffix of the first word?

....

roca que se forma cuando las rocas derretidas se enfrían y endurecen

the color of the powder that a mineral leaves when it is rubbed across a rough surface

Write a sentence using this word.

....

....

....

color del polvo que un mineral deja cuando se lo frota contra una superficie rugosa

rock that forms when sediments are pressed together and cemented

Write a sentence using this word.

....

....

roca que se forma por la acumulación de sedimentos unidos a gran presión

natural resource

recurso natural

silt

limo

metamorphic rock

roca metamórfica

renewable resource

recurso renovable

extinct

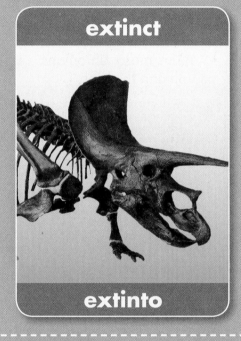

extinto

sieve

criba

nonrenewable resource

recurso no renovable

fossil

fósil

boulder

canto rodado

rock that forms when existing rock is changed by heat and pressure

What is the suffix of the first word?

....

....

roca que se forma cuando las rocas existentes cambian debido al calor y la presión

---

very fine particles of earth and sand carried by moving water

Write a sentence using this word.

....

....

partículas muy finas de tierra y arena que son arrastradas por el agua en movimiento

---

an important material from Earth that living things need

Write a definition using your own words.

....

....

....

un material importante de la Tierra que los seres vivos necesitan

---

a tool used for separating materials

Write a sentence using this word.

....

....

....

instrumento que se usa para separar materiales

---

no longer lives on Earth

Write as many antonyms as you can think of.

....

....

....

....

que ya no existe en la Tierra

---

resource that can be replaced in a fairly short time

Write something that is not an example of this word.

....

....

....

recurso que se puede reemplazar en poco tiempo

---

a large rock that is rounded or worn down by water and weather

Write a definition using your own words.

....

....

roca grande con forma redonda o que está desgastada por el agua o el clima

---

remains or mark of a living thing from long ago

Write a sentence using this word.

....

....

....

restos o marca de un ser vivo que existió hace mucho tiempo

---

resource that cannot be replaced once it is used up

What is the prefix of this word?

....

....

recurso que no se puede reemplazar cuando se acaba

Lesson 1

What are minerals?

- Minerals are natural, nonliving materials that make up rocks.
- Hardness, color, luster, and streak are properties of minerals.

Lesson 2

What are rocks?

- All rocks are made from one or more minerals.
- Different rocks have different physical characteristics.
- Igneous, sedimentary, and metamorphic are types of rock.

Lesson 3

How do you sort rocks?

- Tools, such as sieves, rulers, and scales, can be used to sort different types of rocks based on size.
- Boulders, pebbles, sand, and silt are different types of rocks.

Lesson 4

What can we learn from fossils?

- Fossils help us learn about plants and animals that are extinct.
- By studying characteristics of fossils, scientists learn how plants, animals, and environments have changed.

Lesson 5

What are natural resources?

- Renewable resources are natural resources that are unlimited or easily replaced.
- Nonrenewable resources cannot be replaced.

<table>
<tr><td>

Lesson 1 3.2.2, 3.2.3, 3.2.5, 3.2.6, 3.NS.4, 3.NS.8

</td><td>

Lesson 2 3.2.2, 3.2.6, 3.NS.1, 3.NS.7, 3.NS.8

</td></tr>
</table>

What are minerals?

1. **Conclude** A mineral can be scratched with a coin. What can you conclude about the hardness of the mineral compared to the hardness of the coin?

2. **Explain** What makes a mineral rare?

3. **Define** What is luster?

What are rocks?

4. **Vocabulary** All rocks are made of _____.
   A. clay
   B. minerals
   C. igneous rock
   D. granite

5. **Vocabulary** A(n) _____ rock has been changed by heat and pressure.
   A. igneous
   B. metamorphic
   C. sedimentary
   D. agate

6. **Write About It** What is different about the way igneous rocks and sedimentary rocks form?

Lesson 3   3.2.1, 3.NS.1, 3.NS.5

How do you sort rocks?

7. ◎ **Compare and Contrast** How are a pebble and a piece of sand alike and different?

Lesson 4   3.2.4, 3.NS.8

What can we learn from fossils?

8. **Conclude** Amir studies the characteristics of an animal fossil. The animal appears to have had wings. What can Amir conclude about this animal?

Lesson 5   3.2.5, 3.2.6, 3.NS.7

What are natural resources?

9. **Infer** We get milk from cows and wool from sheep. Are cows and sheep renewable or nonrenewable resources? Why?

10. **APPLY THE BIG ?**   **How do Earth's resources change?**

Describe how people change Earth's resources. Use the terms *renewable* and *nonrenewable*.

Mutliple Choice

1 Look closely at the rock. Which characteristic of this rock helps you know that it is sedimentary rock?

A. color

B. texture

C. layers

D. grains

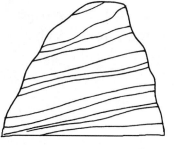

3.2.2

Constructed Response

2 Isabel finds a plant fossil in the desert. It looks like modern plants that live in warm, wet places. What does the fossil tell you about the desert?

....

....

....

....

....

3.2.4

Extended Response

3 Rocks can be classified according to their size. One scale sorts rocks according to their diameters.

Rock Classification by Size	
Type of rock	Diameter (millimeters)
Boulder	greater than 256
Cobble	64-256
Pebble	4-64
Sand	less than 4

What type of rock has a diameter of 357 mm?

....

What do rocks with diameters of 10 mm and 59 mm have in common?

....

Why do you think there is a scale to sort rocks by diameter?

....

....

....

3.2.1

This geochemist is collecting samples outside to research.

3.2.2

Geochemist

Have you ever wondered if water is safe to drink? Geochemists can answer this type of question.

Geochemists study the chemicals that make up Earth materials such as rocks, minerals, water, and oil. Many geochemists work on environmental issues. For example, a geochemist might analyze samples of water and rock from a mine. They could tell if the water is being contaminated and what kinds of rocks are causing the contamination. The geochemist can then help people take steps to clean up the area.

Many other geochemists specialize in finding resources such as minerals. They use their knowledge to help companies obtain these materials. Geochemists try to not damage the environment while they obtain materials.

Geochemists must be good observers and problem solvers. Some of their work takes place in a lab. They also work outside at sites to collect samples. Most geochemists have college and graduate degrees in geology.

 APPLY THE BIG ? How might a geochemist change Earth's resources?

Materials

3 index cards

3 paper plates

plastic cup with gravel

plastic cup with soil

plastic cup with sand

shell

Inquiry Skill In an experiment, you **control variables** by changing only one variable.

Does gravel, sand, or soil make the best imprint?

Sometimes an imprint made by a plant or animal made in the soft ground can become a fossil.

Ask a question.

Which will make the best imprint?

State a hypothesis.

1. Write a **hypothesis.** Circle one choice and finish the sentence.

If imprints are made using gravel, sand, and soil, then the best imprint will be made in

(a) gravel

(b) sand

(c) soil

because

....

Identify and control variables.

2. In an **experiment** you change only one **variable.** Everything else must remain the same. What must stay the same? Give one example.

....

....

3. Tell the one change you will make.

....

....

....

3.2.4 Observe fossils and describe how they provide evidence about the plants and animals that lived long ago and the nature of their environment at that time. **3.NS.2** Design a fair test. **3.NS.9** Compare the results of an investigation with the prediction. **3.DP.6** Create the solution through a prototype. (Also **3.NS.1, 3.DP.9**)

Design your test.

☑ **4.** Draw how you will set up your test.

☑ **5.** List your steps in the order you will do them.

Do your test.

6. Follow the steps you wrote.

7. **Record** your results in the table.

Be careful! **Wash your hands when finished.**

Work Like a Scientist
Scientists test their hypothesis and prediction with multiple trials. Make sure to conduct multiple trials.

Collect and record data.

8. Describe each imprint you made.

Interpret your data.

9. Compare your imprints. Describe how they are alike or different. Explain.

....

....

....

....

State your conclusion.

10. You conducted an **experiment** to test your **hypothesis.**
Compare your hypothesis with your results.
Communicate your conclusions.

....

....

....

....

11. What clues can fossils give about the past?

....

....

....

....

....

....

APPLY THE BIG ?

Unit C Earth Science
Performance-Based Assessment

Investigate Fossils

Obtain samples of several fossils or find pictures of fossils in the library-media center. Find out about the extinct plant or animals that left the fossils. Compare them with living plants or animals.

- If you have fossils, measure each with a metric ruler. Record your data. Write a short description of each fossil.

- Describe features of the fossils that show how extinct plants and animals were like living ones. Describe features that show how they were different from living ones.

- Infer what the environments were like when the extinct plants or animals were alive. Compare those environments with the environments of similar living plants and animals.

3.2.4

Rock Fantasy

Write a fantasy, which is a made-up story, about how an igneous rock changes into a metamorphic rock. Include the following in your fantasy:

- a description of the environment the rock is in

- an explanation of how the rock looks and feels

- a beginning, middle, and ending to the story

3.2.2

Using Scientific Methods

1. Ask a question.
2. State your hypothesis.
3. Identify and control variables.
4. Test your hypothesis.
5. Collect and record your data.
6. Interpret your data.
7. State your conclusion.
8. Go further.

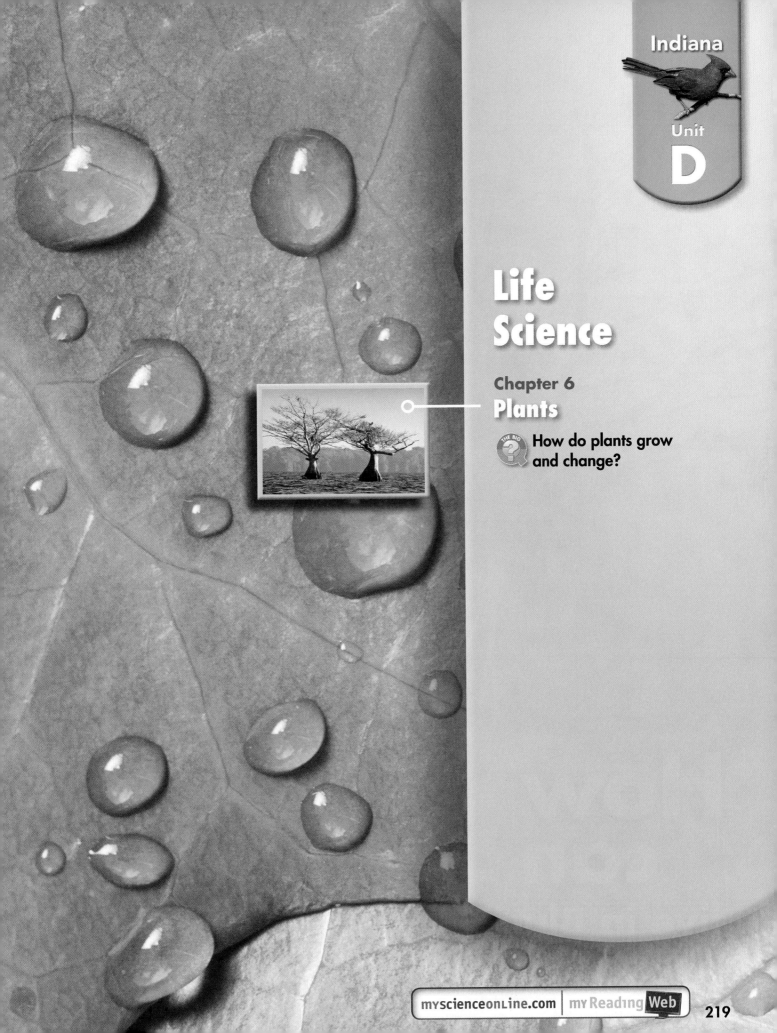

Life Science

Chapter 6
Plants

THE BIG How do plants grow
? and change?

How can trees
live in Blue Cypress Lake?

Plants

Blue Cypress Lake is found in southeastern Florida. Cypress trees can live and grow in slow-moving water.

Predict   How can cypress trees live and grow in water?

....

....

....

How do plants grow and change?

How do plants change?

☐ **1.** Put a wet paper towel in a plastic resealable bag. Add three pinto-bean seeds between the towel and the bag.

☐ **2.** Seal the bag shut. Tape it to a window.

☐ **3. Collect Data** Draw and **record** your **observations** every other day.

Materials

plastic bag

pinto beans

tape

wet paper towels

Day	Observations

Data Table

☐ **4.** Choose a **variable** to change when the seeds grow roots. For example, change the direction of the bag, the amount of light the bag receives, or the temperature inside the bag.

☐ **5. Predict** how your plants will change.

Inquiry Skill
As you observe the growing plants, you **collect data** to show how they change.

Explain Your Results

6. Communicate Explain how your plants reacted to the change.

3.3.1 Observe and identify the common structures of a plant including roots, stems, leaves, flowers, fruits, and seeds, and describe their functions.
3.3.2 Investigate plant growth over time, take measurements in SI units, record the data and display them in graphs. Examine factors that might influence plant growth. **3.NS.1** Make predictions and formulate testable questions. (Also **3.NS.2, 3.DP.9**)

⊙ Text Features

Text features, such as headings, highlighting, pictures, and captions, give you clues about what you will read.

A **heading** tells what the content that follows is about.

A **picture** shows something you will read about.

A **caption** tells specific information about a picture.

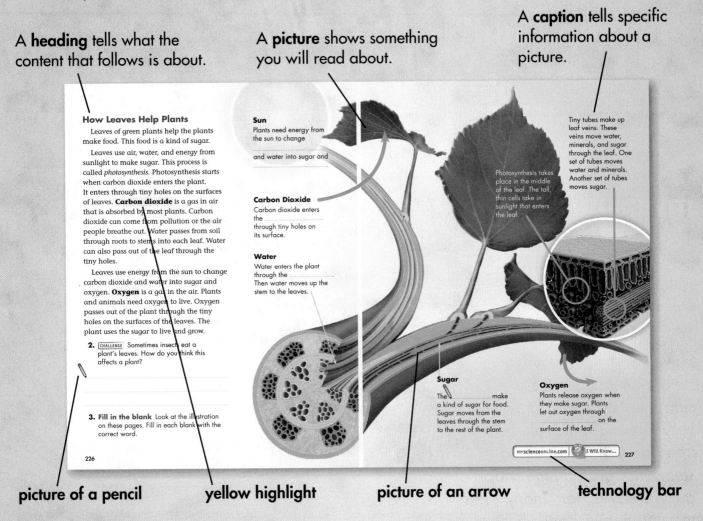

How Leaves Help Plants

Leaves of green plants help the plants make food. This food is a kind of sugar.

Leaves use air, water, and energy from sunlight to make sugar. This process is called *photosynthesis*. Photosynthesis starts when carbon dioxide enters the plant. It enters through tiny holes on the surfaces of leaves. **Carbon dioxide** is a gas in air that is absorbed by most plants. Carbon dioxide can come from pollution or the air people breathe out. Water passes from soil through roots to stems into each leaf. Water can also pass out of the leaf through the tiny holes.

Leaves use energy from the sun to change carbon dioxide and water into sugar and oxygen. **Oxygen** is a gas in the air. Plants and animals need oxygen to live. Oxygen passes out of the plant through the tiny holes on the surfaces of the leaves. The plant uses the sugar to live and grow.

2. CHALLENGE Sometimes insects eat a plant's leaves. How do you think this affects a plant?

3. **Fill in the blank** Look at the illustration on these pages. Fill in each blank with the correct word.

226

Sun
Plants need energy from the sun to change _____ and water into sugar and _____

Carbon Dioxide
Carbon dioxide enters the _____ through tiny holes on its surface.

Water
Water enters the plant through the _____. Then water moves up the stem to the leaves.

Photosynthesis takes place in the middle of the leaf. The tall, thin cells take in sunlight that enters the leaf.

Tiny tubes make up leaf veins. These veins move water, minerals, and sugar through the leaf. One set of tubes moves water and minerals. Another set of tubes moves sugar.

Sugar
The _____ make a kind of sugar for food. Sugar moves from the leaves through the stem to the rest of the plant.

Oxygen
Plants release oxygen when they make sugar. Plants let out oxygen through _____ on the surface of the leaf.

myscienceonline.com I Will Know... 227

picture of a pencil

yellow highlight

picture of an arrow

technology bar

Practice It!

Read the text features in the chart below. Find the text features in the textbook pages shown above. Write a clue that each one gives you about the content.

Text feature	Clue
yellow highlight	
picture of a pencil	
technology bar	

How do plants use sunlight to make food?

3.3.1 Observe and identify the common structures of a plant including roots, stems, leaves, flowers, fruits, and seeds, and describe their functions.
3.NS.3 Plan and carry out investigations as a class, in small groups or independently, often over a period of several class lessons. (Also **3.NS.8**)

Tell how you think leaves help plants.

my planet diary

FunFact

Have you raked leaves before? Many leaves are small. Other leaves grow very large. The traveler's tree has giant leaves and stems that grow in the shape of a fan. Leaves from many trees may fit in your hand, but not the leaves of the traveler's tree! The leaves on a traveler's tree grow to be up to three meters long. That's more than two times larger than an adult human! The base of each leaf can also hold about one liter of water. This tree is native to an island off the coast of Africa. This island is called Madagascar. However, the traveler's tree grows in warm places around the world like southeastern Florida.

Infer Why do you think this is called a traveler's tree?

....

....

....

....

....

myscienceonline.com | 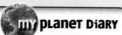 my planet diary

I will know that leaves help plants live, grow, and make food.

Words to Know

carbon dioxide
oxygen

What Plants Need

Plants need food, air, water, and space to live and grow. Plants live and grow in soil. The four main parts of a plant are leaves, roots, stems, and flowers. In different kinds of plants, these parts may look alike. They may also look different.

Unlike animals, plants make their own food. Plants need energy from the sun to make food. Energy from the sun enters leaves and helps plants make food. This food helps plants grow.

1. ◎ **Text Features** Look at the text features on this page. Identify one text feature and the clue it gives you.

Bromeliad plants are like other plants. They use energy from the sun to make food.

Text feature	Clue
Heading	It tells what I'll read about.

How Leaves Help Plants

Leaves of green plants help the plants make food. This food is a kind of sugar.

Leaves use air, water, and energy from sunlight to make sugar. This process is called *photosynthesis*. Photosynthesis starts when carbon dioxide enters the plant. It enters through tiny holes on the surfaces of leaves. **Carbon dioxide** is a gas in air that is absorbed by most plants. Carbon dioxide can come from pollution or the air people breathe out. Water passes from soil through roots to stems into each leaf. Water can also pass out of the leaf through the tiny holes.

Leaves use energy from the sun to change carbon dioxide and water into sugar and oxygen. **Oxygen** is a gas in the air. Plants and animals need oxygen to live. Oxygen passes out of the plant through the tiny holes on the surfaces of the leaves. The plant uses the sugar to live and grow.

2. CHALLENGE Sometimes insects eat a plant's leaves. How do you think this affects a plant?

....

....

....

3. Fill in the blank Look at the illustration on these pages. Fill in each blank with the correct word.

Sun

Plants need energy from the sun to change

....

and water into sugar and

....

Carbon Dioxide

Carbon dioxide enters the .... through tiny holes on its surface.

Water

Water enters the plant through the .... Then water moves up the stem to the leaves.

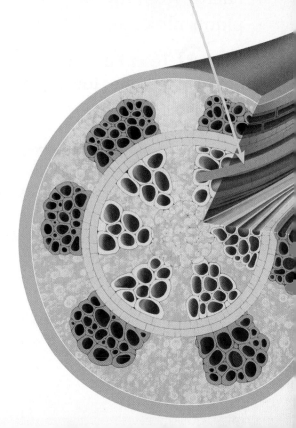

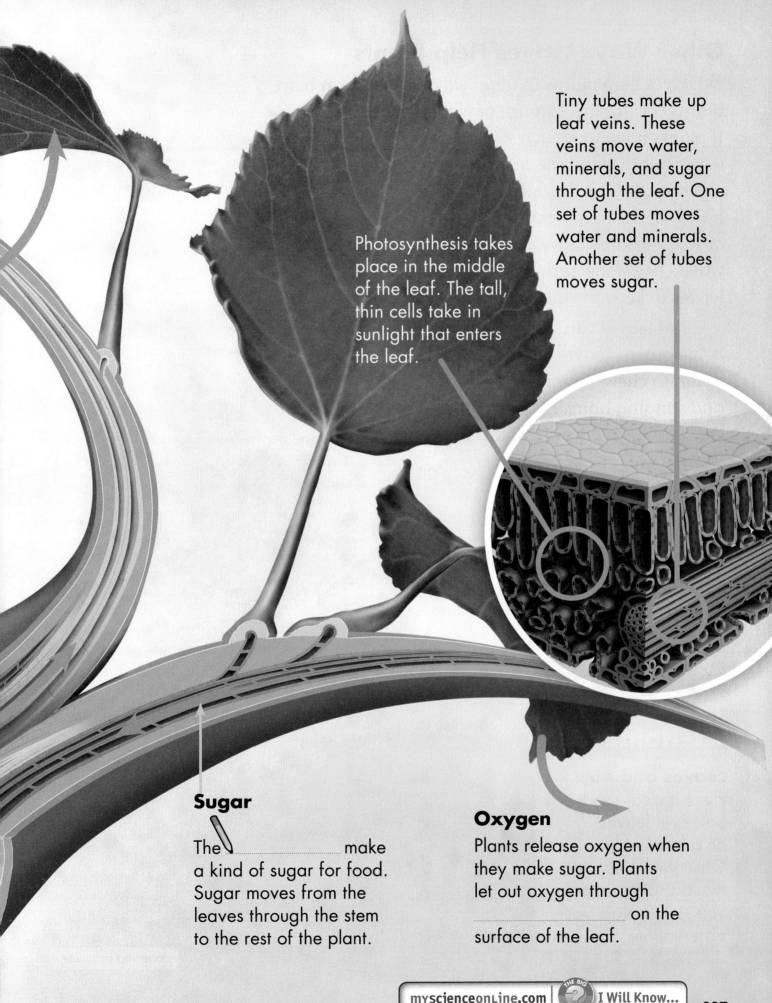

Photosynthesis takes place in the middle of the leaf. The tall, thin cells take in sunlight that enters the leaf.

Tiny tubes make up leaf veins. These veins move water, minerals, and sugar through the leaf. One set of tubes moves water and minerals. Another set of tubes moves sugar.

Sugar

The _____ make a kind of sugar for food. Sugar moves from the leaves through the stem to the rest of the plant.

Oxygen

Plants release oxygen when they make sugar. Plants let out oxygen through _____ on the surface of the leaf.

Other Ways Leaves Help Plants

Leaves help plants in other ways. Leaves can help plants control the amount of water in the plant. If plants have too much water, leaves let some water out through the tiny holes on their surfaces. A plant can also stop water loss by closing these holes. Plants in dry environments may have waxy- or fuzzy- coated leaves. This coating helps keep in water. The stonecrop succulent has waxy-coated leaves to keep in water.

Plant leaves can also protect the plant from being eaten. Leaves can be poisonous, sharp, or tough to chew. Sharp leaves include thorns, spines, and stinging hairs. Hungry animals may not eat a cactus plant with sharp leaves.

4. **Identify** List two ways a leaf can help a plant.

....

....

....

At-Home Lab

Leaves and Air
Place a clear sandwich bag over leaves on a tree branch. Observe the bag for two days. Tell what you see. Explain your observations.

stonecrop succulent

myscienceonline.com | Got it? 60-Second Video

5. Draw Think about a plant in your neighborhood. Draw a leaf from this plant. Describe to a partner how you think the leaf helps the plant.

Poison ivy is a woody vine. It is found in forests across North America. Poison ivy causes an itchy rash, blistering, and burning of the skin.

Got it?

🟡 3.3.1, 3.NS.3, 3.NS.8

6. List five things plants need to make food.

....

....

7. **UNLOCK THE BIG ?** Think about what you learned about plant leaves in this lesson. How do plants grow and change?

....

....

....

⬛ **Stop!** I need help with ....

⏸ **Wait!** I have a question about ....

▶ **Go!** Now I know ....

How do plants use roots and stems to grow?

🔵 3.3.1 Observe and identify the common structures of a plant including roots, stems, leaves, flowers, fruits, and seeds, and describe their functions.
3.NS.1 Make predictions and formulate testable questions.

Circle, in different colors, the roots, stems, and leaves of these mangrove trees.

Inquiry **Explore It!**

Which way will roots grow?

☐ **1.** Fold and place the towels in the cup. Wet the towels.

☐ **2.** Place the seeds in different directions.

☐ **3. Observe** the seeds every day for one week. Watch the way the roots grow.

Materials

2 paper towels

plastic cup

water

4 bean seeds

Explain Your Results

4. Infer Write what you learned about the way roots grow.

....

....

myscienceonline.com | **Explore It!** Animation

🔵 3.3.2 Investigate plant growth over time, take measurements in SI units, record the data and display them in graphs. Examine factors that might influence plant growth. (Also **3.NS.3, 3.NS.8**)

I will know how roots and stems take in, transport, or store water and nutrients the plant needs to grow.

Word to Know

nutrient

How Roots Help Plants

Look at all the roots of the fir tree in the picture. Plants need roots and stems to take in and move materials the plant needs to live and grow.

The root system of a plant is often below the ground. You cannot usually see it. Roots keep the plant stable in the ground. Roots store food made by the plant's leaves. Roots also take in water and materials called minerals from the soil. The plant gets nutrients from the water and minerals. A **nutrient** is any material needed by living things for energy, growth, and repair. Plants need nutrients to live and grow.

1. **Determine** Look at the picture of the fir tree roots. What would happen if the plant's roots did not store food?

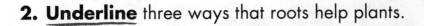

2. **Underline** three ways that roots help plants.

Fir tree roots take in nutrients from the soil.

Types of Roots

Have you ever eaten a carrot? Many plants have one large root called a *taproot*. Carrots and dandelions are examples of taproots. Taproots grow deep into the soil toward Earth's center due to gravity. Taproots take in water and nutrients from the soil. The roots also store food made by the plant.

In some plants, such as grass and pine trees, roots spread out in many directions. This type of root is called a *fibrous root*. Like taproots, fibrous roots store food, take in water and nutrients, and grow toward Earth's center due to gravity. Fibrous roots of the same plant are all about the same size. They grow longer than taproots. Fibrous roots also grow close to the surface to take in water after it rains.

root hair

3. Fill in the blank Look at the illustration of the root. Fill in each blank with the correct word.

_____ enters the root through the root hairs. All roots have root hairs. The more root hairs a plant has, the more water the plant can take in. Roots with many root hairs grow far into the soil to reach water and _____ .

4. [CHALLENGE] Which type of roots could help a plant more in a dry area—a fibrous root or a taproot?

pumpkin stem

5. Analyze What is the role of pumpkin's stem?

....

....

....

....

....

How Stems Help Plants

Stems support the leaves, flowers, and fruits of plants. Stems often grow up toward the light, their main source of energy. Most plant stems have tiny tubes that move water and minerals from the roots to the leaves. Other tubes move food from the leaves to the stems and roots.

Some stems are thin and grow along the surface of the ground. For example, the stem of a pumpkin can grow roots and a new plant. Other stems, called vines, grow parts that wrap around objects that support the plant. Ivy is a vine that grows on the ground or on buildings.

Lightning Lab

Look at Plant Roots
Work with an adult. Cut a carrot in half. Look at the cross section. List what structures you see. Try this with another root. On the same paper, list the structures of the other root.

Types of Stems

Plant stems come in many different shapes, sizes, and colors. Some stems grow below ground. Other stems such as this cactus stem grow above ground. Notice how thick cactus stems can grow. Cactus stems swell up to store water. As the cactus uses stored water due to heat, the stems shrink. Cactus stems are thick and waxy. This keeps them from losing water. Cactus stems help them survive in a desert.

6. ◉ **Text Features**
Which text features on this page help you understand different types of stems?

....

....

....

More water makes stems swell outward.

Water from roots is stored in this area.

The spines growing out of this cactus stem are a special kind of leaf.

Water from roots moves up these tubes.

Parts of some stems grow below ground. Have you eaten a potato? You eat the part of the stem that stored food below ground. Stems that grow below ground can make new stems from buds, such as the potato's "eyes." These buds grow up out of the ground and become new plants.

7. **Support** Look at the cactus stem and potato. How do these stems help each plant?

....

....

....

....

Got it? ⏺ 3.3.1, 3.NS.1

8. **Hypothesize** How could a plant grow in soil without many minerals?

....

....

....

9. **Describe** Why do roots grow toward Earth's center?

....

....

⏹ **Stop!** I need help with ....

⏸ **Wait!** I have a question about ....

▶ **Go!** Now I know ....

Lesson 3
What affects plant growth?

3.3.2 Investigate plant growth over time, take measurements in SI units, record the data and display them in graphs. Examine factors that might influence plant growth. 3.NS.3 Plan and carry out investigations as a class, in small groups or independently, often over a period of several class lessons. (Also 3.NS.1, 3.NS.5, 3.NS.7)

Tell how you think the weather will affect these peonies.

Inquiry Explore It!

What do plants need to be healthy?

☐ **1.** Put 10 seeds in Cup A. Put 80 seeds in Cup B.

☐ **2.** Cover the seeds with soil. Add 4 spoonfuls of water. Put the cups in sunlight. Add 1 spoonful of water every day.

☐ **3. Observe** the stems and leaves. Compare how they look after 3 weeks.

Materials

90 radish seeds

spoon

plastic cup with water

A B 2 paper cups with soil

Explain Your Results

4. Which cup has healthier looking plants?

5. Draw a Conclusion What is one thing plants need to be healthy?

3.3.1 Observe and identify the common structures of a plant including roots, stems, leaves, flowers, fruits, and seeds, and describe their functions. 3.NS.8 Identify simple patterns in data and propose explanations to account for the patterns.

mYscienceonLine.com | **Explore It!** Animation

Word to Know

fertilizer

Factors of Plant Growth

Plants are like other living things. Plants use energy, respond to their environment, and grow. Many things can affect plant growth.

Seasons and temperature can affect plant growth. For example, plants grow more quickly during summer than winter. This happens because many plants produce food to grow when temperatures are warm. Some plants then use stored food to survive when temperatures are cold. Their growth slows until spring comes and temperatures begin to warm.

1. **Hypothesize** Why might some plants grow at a steady rate?

....

....

....

2. **Infer** What else might affect plant growth?

....

....

....

The growth of this rose slows when temperatures are cold.

3. **Investigate** How could you use measurement to study plant growth?

4. **Hypothesize** What might happen if a plant had plenty of potassium but very little water?

At-Home Lab

Sun Garden
Measure the growth of a plant in millimeters every day for one week. Record your measurements in a graph. Predict how more or less sunlight might affect plant growth.

Plant Growth and Nutrients

Living things need more than warm temperatures to live and grow. Plants also need nutrients. For example, plants use the nutrients carbon, oxygen, and hydrogen to produce food. Plants get carbon and oxygen from the air. Plants get hydrogen from water in soil. Plant roots take in the water.

Plant roots take in other nutrients such as nitrogen, potassium, and phosphorus from soil. These three nutrients are common in plant fertilizers. **Fertilizer** is a substance added to soil to help the plant produce more food.

Nitrogen keeps plants healthy. Nitrogen is a gas that makes up about four-fifths of the air around us. Yet most plants cannot get nitrogen from the air. Most plants get nitrogen through the soil. Nitrogen provides structure to parts of plants. It also helps plants produce food and reproduce. Plants will not grow if nitrogen is not present.

Potassium helps regulate water in plants. It keeps water in the leaves. This helps plants survive when water is scarce. Phosphorus is important for plant growth. It helps convert energy from the sun to chemical energy. This happens when plants produce food.

The nutrients in fertilizer help plants grow.

myscienceonline.com | Got it? | 60-Second Video

Sunlight helps Indiana crops such as corn grow.

Plant Growth and Sunlight

Energy from the sun allows plants to use nutrients to produce food. Plants grow toward sunlight. Some plants change position during the day so their leaves can be in direct sunlight. Many plants could not survive without sunlight.

Got it?

🔘 3.3.2, 3.NS.1, 3.NS.3, 3.NS.5, 3.NS.7

5. Explain Describe where plants get nutrients and how they use them.

....

....

....

6. Examine List three factors that affect plant growth.

....

....

⬛ **Stop!** I need help with ....

⏸ **Wait!** I have a question about ....

▶ **Go!** Now I know ....

Lesson 4

How do plants use flowers or cones to reproduce?

3.3.1 Observe and identify the common structures of a plant including roots, stems, leaves, flowers, fruits, and seeds, and describe their functions. 3.NS.8 Identify simple patterns in data and propose explanations to account for the patterns. (Also 3.NS.7)

Circle what is helping these plants make new plants.

Inquiry **Explore It!**

What are the parts of a flower?

Some plants use flowers to reproduce.
The flowers make seeds that grow into new plants.

☐ **1. Observe** and draw a flower. As you read the lesson, identify the parts and describe their functions.

Materials

flower

colored pencils

hand lens

Explain Your Results

2. Interpret Data Compare your drawings with those made by others. How are they alike and different?

....

....

scienceonline.com | **Explore It!** Animation

3.3.1 Observe and identify the common structures of a plant including roots, stems, leaves, flowers, fruits, and seeds, and describe their functions.

I will know how plants reproduce using seeds and cones.

Words to Know

reproduce
pollinate
germinate

Reproduction

Most plants make seeds that grow into new plants. Some plants grow stems or roots that grow into a new plant. Plants can reproduce both ways. When plants **reproduce,** they make more of the same kind. For example, maple trees produce seeds. These seeds can grow into new maple trees.

Each seed carries information from the parent plants. The seed uses this information and food stored from the parent plant in the seed to grow into a new plant. The new plant will be like its parents. After seeds are produced, they may scatter or move away from the parent plant. This gives the new plant more room to grow.

1. **Predict** What may happen if seeds do not scatter?

2. **Determine** Each seed in the picture below has a tiny parachute. How do you think these parachutes help the seeds scatter?

seed with parachute

Parts of a Flower

Flowering plants grow flowers that make seeds. Flowers have different parts. One part makes pollen. Another part, the petals, attracts bees and other animals to the flower. Animals or wind can **pollinate**, or carry pollen to, another flower. Pollination happens when animals or wind move pollen to the part of the flower that makes seeds. After pollination, seeds form near the center of the flower. Another part, fruit, often grows around the seed to protect it. A peach is an example of a fruit.

3. ◉ **Text Features** Tell what these captions helped you learn about plant reproduction.

4. **Summarize** What is the function of one part of a flower?

....

....

....

....

....

....

Pollen sticks to the bodies of bees as bees look for food. Bees carry this pollen to the part of another flower that makes seeds.

A flower's colorful petals attract insects and other animals that pollinate the flower.

The tip of this part of the flower makes pollen.

Pollen helps form seeds.

myscienceonline.com | THE BIG ? | I Will Know...

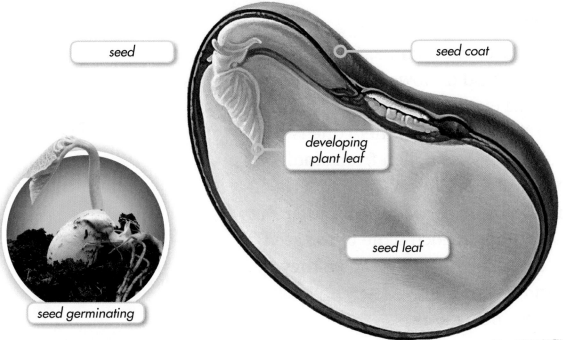

seed

seed coat

developing plant leaf

seed leaf

seed germinating

How Seeds Grow

Seeds have different shapes, sizes, and colors. All seeds have the same parts. Every seed has material inside it that can grow into a new plant. The seed is covered by a seed coat. The seed coat protects this material. Many seeds have one seed leaf or two seed leaves. As it grows, the tiny plant uses food from the seed.

Seeds need air, the right amount of water, and the right temperature to **germinate,** or begin to grow. With the right conditions, the young plant, or seedling, germinates. The seedling uses food stored in the seed to grow.

As the seedling grows, it grows out of the soil. Leaves grow from the stem. The leaves use sunlight to make sugar. The plant uses the sugar for food. The seedling can grow into an adult plant that has flowers. The flowers are pollinated and new seeds form. If these new seeds germinate, they can grow into new plants. Then the cycle begins again.

5. CHALLENGE Look at the illustration of the seed. Why do you think the seed coat is important?

....

....

....

At-Home Lab

Plant Detective
Work with an adult. Cut open 3 different fruits. Observe and identify the parts of the fruit. Compare the seeds. Count them. How were the fruits and seeds alike and different? Share your observations.

How Cones Help Plants

Cones are made by conifer plants. Conifer plants grow cones instead of flowers to make seeds. Conifers make two types of cones. One cone is a small pollen cone. The other cone is a large seed cone. Wind blows pollen from small pollen cones to large seed cones. When pollen sticks to the large seed cones, seeds begin to grow inside. A seed grows under each scale of the seed cone. When the seeds are fully developed, they float to the ground. If conditions are right, each seed can grow into a new plant.

6. **Describe** What happens after the seed in a cone is fully developed?

7. **State** Write a caption for the photo below.

First, wind blows pollen from these small cones to larger cones on other trees.

Next, seeds begin to grow inside the cones.

myscienceonline.com | Got *it?* 60-Second Video

Do the math!

Elapsed Time

If you plant a green bean seed, when can you eat green beans? You can eat them when fruit ripens. Different plants have different lengths of time from seed to fruit. Use the table and calendars to answer the questions.

1 **Solve** If you plant cucumber seeds on May 21, when can you eat cucumbers?

2 **Solve** If you eat ripe tomatoes on July 29, when were the seeds planted?

Days from Seed to Fruit

green bean seeds	58 days
cucumber seeds	55 days
tomato seeds	59 days

Got it?

🔵 3.3.1, 3.NS.7, 3.NS.8

8. Analyze What role do seeds and cones play in plant reproduction?

....

....

9. **UNLOCK THE BIG ?** Think about what you learned in this lesson. How do plants grow and change?

....

....

⬛ **Stop!** I need help with ....

⏸ **Wait!** I have a question about ....

▶ **Go!** Now I know ....

How do you classify plants?

3.3.1 Observe and identify the common structures of a plant including roots, stems, leaves, flowers, fruits, and seeds, and describe their functions. 3.NS.7 Keep accurate records in a notebook during investigations and communicate findings to others using graphs, charts, maps and models through oral and written reports.

Envision It!

Tell which characteristics you think can help you classify each plant.

my planet diary

Science Stats

Statistics are pieces of information that can help us answer questions. Statistics can help us determine the oldest known living plant. In 2004, scientists in Sweden discovered tree roots that are about 9,550 years old. The tree they found is called a Norway spruce. It is only 4 meters tall. The part of the tree you see is not very old. The roots of the tree are old. Each time the tree above ground dies, a new tree starts growing from the roots.

Which trees have lived above ground the longest? The oldest trees above ground are most likely bristlecone pine trees. One bristlecone pine tree in California is almost 5,000 years old.

What is the oldest part of the oldest tree in the world?

....

Underline the statistic that tells about the age of the Norway spruce.

bristlecone pine tree

I will know how to classify plants into major groups based on the physical characteristics of the plants.

Words to Know

flowering plant
spore

Classify Plants

At grocery stores, people sort food into groups. This helps shoppers find the right foods. Scientists classify living things, such as plants, in a similar way. Scientists classify plants by sorting them into groups. This helps us identify plants.

You can classify plants into groups by color, size, and shape. Use these steps to help classify plants. First, look at the leaf size and shape of the plant. Next, find out if the plant grows flowers or does not grow flowers. Finally, find out if the plant makes seeds or does not make seeds.

1. ⊙ **Sequence** Complete the graphic organizer to show the sequence of classifying plants.

First

Look at the plant leaf size and shape.

Next

Finally

2. **Classify** These water lilies have large leaves that float on water. What is another way you can classify these water lilies?

Flowering Plants

One way to classify plants is by whether or not a plant produces flowers. An orange tree and a cactus do not look alike, but they are both flowering plants. **Flowering plants** are plants with seeds that grow flowers. Orange trees grow flowers with seeds. These seeds can grow into a new plant.

There are different groups of flowering plants. Each group has different kinds of roots, stems, leaves, and flowers. For example, a dogwood tree has a stiff, woody stem. These stems help dogwoods grow tall. Iris plants do not have woody stems. Iris plants grow closer to the ground.

Leaves fall off dogwood trees in the fall. The leaves grow back in the spring. A tree that loses and grows leaves like this is called a *deciduous* tree.

3. Circle the words that tell about flowering plants.

4. ⊙ **Text Features** Why does the word *deciduous* look different from other words on this page?

....

....

Dogwood trees can grow taller than six meters. Dogwoods produce flowers. These flowers make seeds. The seeds can grow into new dogwoods.

Groups of Flowering Plants

One kind of flowering plant is the magnolia tree. It produces colorful flowers. Some magnolias are deciduous. Others keep their leaves all winter. Magnolia trees have strong, woody stems. These stems help magnolias grow tall. They range in height from shorter than three meters to taller than twenty meters.

Iris plants grow long, thin stems and leaves. These stems allow iris plants to bend when winds blow against them. Iris plants lose both stems and leaves in the fall. The roots live through the winter. The stems and leaves grow back from the roots in spring. During the spring, iris plants produce colorful flowers.

Rosebushes are another kind of flowering plant. They grow as small shrubs or long vines. Rose stems are strong and have sharp prickles. These stems allow rosebushes to grow large. The prickles protect the plant. Most rose flowers are colorful.

5. ⊚ **Compare and Contrast** Look at the flowering plants on this page. How are they alike and different?

....

....

6. **Evaluate** What is an advantage of a thin stem?

....

Nonflowering Plants

Some kinds of plants do not grow flowers to make seeds. *Coniferous* trees grow cones instead of flowers to make seeds. Seeds grow inside each cone. Cones fall from coniferous trees to spread seeds. These seeds can make new plants.

The leaves of most coniferous trees look like needles or brushes. Most coniferous trees do not lose all their leaves in the fall. Pine and spruce trees are types of coniferous trees.

7. **Word Structure** The word *coniferous* is made up of the base word *conifer*, which means "cone-bearing," and the suffix *-ous,* which means "full of." Why do you think trees that grow cones are called coniferous trees?

8. **Hypothesize** Write why you think these cones have scales all around them.

cones

Spores

Ferns and mosses are two kinds of plants that do not make seeds. They reproduce by making spores. A **spore** is a small cell that grows into a new plant. Mosses produce spores at the end of their stalks. Ferns produce spores on the undersides of their leaves.

Mosses and ferns reproduce by making spores.

spore

fern

moss

9. Distinguish How are spores and seeds different from cones?

....

....

....

....

10. Classify Look at the three plants to the right. How would you classify each plant?

....

....

....

....

Rain Forest Plants

Flowering and nonflowering plants grow and reproduce in rain forests. Some flowering and nonflowering plants produce flowers, seeds, cones, or spores.

11. Categorize What kinds of plants do you see in this picture?

....

....

....

12. Classify Find one plant in this rain forest. Describe two physical characteristics of the plant. How would you classify this plant?

....

....

....

....

myscienceonLine.com | Got it? 60-Second Video

Got it? 📕 3.3.1, 3.NS.7

13. **Classify** How would you classify an unknown plant that does not have flowers?

....

....

14. **UNLOCK THE BIG ?** Think about what you learned about plants in this lesson. How do we classify living things?

....

....

....

⬛ **Stop!** I need help with ....

⏸ **Wait!** I have a question about ....

▶ **Go!** Now I know ....

How does a radish grow?

Follow a Procedure

☑ **1.** Fill a cup with soil to within 2 cm of the top.

☑ **2.** Push 3 radish seeds 1 cm below the soil surface.

☑ **3.** Place the cup in a sunny place. Add 20 mL of water.

☑ **4.** Cover the cup with plastic wrap.

☑ **5.** About every two days, **observe** and add 15 mL of water. On Day 3, remove the plastic wrap. When green plants appear, **record** their heights in the table. Observe for about 9 days.

Materials

3 radish seeds

paper cup

graduated cylinder

soil

plastic wrap

metric ruler

Inquiry Skill When you collect data, you can use a table to **record** observations.

Be careful! **Wash your hands when finished!**

3.3.2 Investigate plant growth over time, take measurements in SI units, record the data and display them in graphs. Examine factors that might influence plant growth. **3.4.1** Choose and use appropriate tools to estimate and measure length, mass, and temperature in SI units. **3.DP.9** Present evidence using mathematical representations (graphs, data tables). (Also **3.NS.5**, **3.NS.7**)

Plant Heights (cm)			
	Plant A	Plant B	Plant C
Day 1 (Day seeds are planted.)	0	0	0
Day			
Day			
Day			
Day			

Analyze and Conclude

6. Observe On which day did a plant first appear?

....

7. Choose one plant in your cup. Make a graph showing the change in height over time.

Plant Growth Over Time

Plant ....

Plant Height (cm): 8, 6, 4, 2, 0

Day 1 ....

Days

8. How did your seeds change?

....

....

Botanical Illustrator

🔵 3.3.1

Do you like to draw? If so, perhaps you would like to be a botanical illustrator. A botanical illustrator draws or paints plants to show what they look like. To draw plants well, you have to be a good observer of nature. This way you can show the details that make plants different. When you draw, you must show the right size and shape of each plant part.

To be a botanical illustrator, you need a degree from a college or art school. Most of your classes would be in art. Some of your classes might also be in biology. You could work for a museum or botanical garden. You might draw illustrations to be used in science books or nature-reserve brochures.

Heeyoung Kim is a botanical illustrator who paints wildflowers. She researches each flower before painting it. Heeyoung Kim wants people to see the beauty of flowers.

Illustrate What did you learn in this chapter that can help you draw detailed images of how a plant grows and changes?

....

....

....

Vocabulary Smart Cards

carbon dioxide
oxygen
nutrient
fertilizer
reproduce
pollinate
germinate
flowering plant
spore

Play a Game!

Cut out the Vocabulary Smart Cards.

Work with a partner. Spread out the Vocabulary Smart Cards on a table. Have one partner pick a card. Use the word in a sentence. Refer to the definition if you are not familiar with the word.

Have your partner repeat with another Vocabulary Smart Card.

fertilizer

fertilizante

carbon dioxide

dióxido de carbono

reproduce

reproducir

oxygen

oxígeno

pollinate

polinizar

nutrient

nutriente

Interactive Vocabulary

Make a Word Frame!

Choose a vocabulary word and write it in the center of the frame. Write or draw details about the vocabulary word in the spaces around it.

a gas in air that is absorbed by some plants

Write a sentence using this term.

....

....

....

gas en el aire que algunas plantas absorben

---

a substance added to soil to help the plant produce more food

Write a definition using your own words.

....

....

....

sustancia que se agrega al suelo para que la planta produzca más alimento

---

a gas in the air that plants and animals need to live

Write a sentence using this word.

....

....

gas en el aire que las plantas y los animales necesitan para vivir

---

to make more of the same kind

Write the noun form of this word.

....

....

....

hacer más de una misma cosa

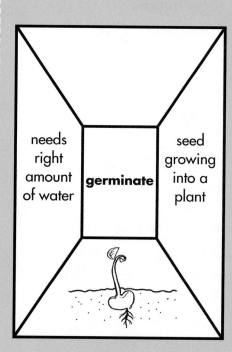

needs right amount of water — **germinate** — seed growing into a plant

---

any material needed by living things for energy, growth, and repair

Write two other forms of this word.

....

....

cualquier sustancia que los seres vivos necesitan para obtener energía, crecer y reponerse

---

to carry pollen to

Draw an example.

llevar polen de un lugar a otro

germinate

germinar

flowering plant

angiosperma

spore

espora

to begin to grow

Draw an example.

empezar a crecer

---

a plant with seeds that grows flowers

Draw an example.

planta con semillas que produce flores

---

a small cell that grows into a new plant

Write a sentence using this word.

....

....

....

célula pequeña que se convierte en una planta nueva

Lesson 1

How do plants use sunlight to make food?

- Leaves use air, water, and energy from the sun to make food for plants. This process is called photosynthesis.
- Leaves can help control the amount of water in a plant.

Lesson 2

How do plants use roots and stems to grow?

- Roots hold the plant in the ground and store food.
- Stems support and protect plants.
- Roots and stems take in and move materials in a plant.

Lesson 3

What affects plant growth?

- Temperature and sunlight influence plant growth.
- Plants use nutrients, such as potassium and phosphorus, to produce food and grow.

Lesson 4

How do plants use flowers or cones to reproduce?

- Some plants can reproduce using seeds or cones.
- A seed has material inside it that can grow into a new plant.
- If conditions are right, a seed can germinate into a seedling.

Lesson 5

How do you classify plants?

- Plants can be classified according to their characteristics, such as flowering and nonflowering.
- Some plants make seeds and some plants make spores.

Chapter Review

How do plants grow and change?

Lesson 1 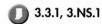 3.3.1, 3.NS.3, 3.NS.8

How do plants use sunlight to make food?

1. **Vocabulary** Plants need a gas in the air called _____ to make sugar.
   A. oxygen
   B. nitrogen
   C. carbon dioxide
   D. mineral

2. **Text Features** What do captions for pictures in a lesson tell you?

3. **Decide** What is one thing a plant must do before it can make sugar and oxygen?

Lesson 2 3.3.1, 3.NS.1

How do plants use roots and stems to grow?

4. **Analyze** Describe one way stems help a plant.

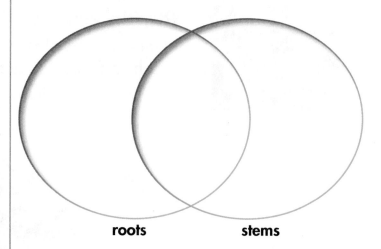

5. **Compare and Contrast** How are roots and stems alike and different?

roots   stems

Lesson 3   3.3.2, 3.NS.1, 3.NS.3, 3.NS.5, 3.NS.7

What affects plant growth?

6. **Summarize** What do plants need in order to grow?

....

....

....

....

....

....

Lesson 4   3.3.1, 3.NS.7, 3.NS.8

How do plants use flowers or cones to reproduce?

7. **Infer** Bees help pollinate apple trees. How might a disease that kills bees affect the number of apple trees? Explain.

....

....

....

....

Lesson 5   3.3.1, 3.NS.7

How do you classify plants?

8. **Write About It** How would you classify a plant if you had never seen it before?

....

....

....

....

....

....

9. **APPLY THE BIG** **How do plants grow and change?**

Use the terms *carbon dioxide*, *oxygen*, and *nutrient* to describe how plants grow and change.

....

....

....

....

....

Multiple Choice

1 Leaves turn carbon dioxide and water into what two things?

A. sugar and oxygen

B. seedlings and sugar

C. oxygen and stems

D. nutrients and sugar

⬤ 3.3.1

Constructed Response

2 How are roots and leaves important to a plant?

....

....

....

....

....

....

⬤ 3.3.1

Extended Response

3 Carlos wanted to compare the growth rates of two plants. In one cup, he planted a pinto bean seed. In another cup, he planted a basil seed. He measured and recorded their heights every other day during a period of 10 days.

Height Grown by Different Plants

Day	Pinto bean (millimeters)	Basil (millimeters)
2	13	8
4	33	29
6	63	53
8	75	61
10	85	68

Which plant grew highest after 10 days?

....

Which plant grew more between Day 2 and Day 4?

....

Did the plants grow more at the beginning or end of the 10 day test?

....

....

⬤ 3.3.2

International Space Station

Field Trip

What if astronauts run out of food during long space missions? They grow more on the ship! NASA researchers have tested ways to grow wheat aboard the International Space Station (ISS). They also test the ability of plants to clean the air and water that astronauts use.

Scientists use a greenhouse on the ISS to test plant growth in space.

Growing plants in space is tricky, however. When seeds germinate on Earth, roots grow down and stems grow up. In space, there is no up or down. As a plant researcher you might be asked to solve problems like this one.

Plant researchers at Kennedy Space Center help prepare experiments to go to the International Space Station. They also study the findings of the astronauts at the space station. You can visit plant researchers at Kennedy Space Center to learn more.

Infer What other problems need to be solved so that plants can grow in space?

....

....

....

Materials

3 paper towels

aluminum foil

waxed paper

tape

graduated cylinder

water

Inquiry Skill
Every experiment must have a **hypothesis,** a testable statement.

How can plants survive in the desert?

Some plants have flat leaves. Many cactus plants have leaves shaped like needles. Some leaves have a waxy coating. The shape of the leaf helps the plant survive.

Ask a question.

How can a leaf's structure help a plant hold water?

State a hypothesis.

1. Write a **hypothesis.** Circle one choice and finish the sentence. If a leaf is narrow and thin and has a waxy coating, it will lose water

a) more slowly
b) more quickly

than flat leaves or leaves without a waxy coating because

....

....

....

Identify and control variables.

2. In an **experiment** you change only one **variable.** Everything else must remain the same. What must stay the same? Give one example.

....

....

3. Tell the one change you will make.

....

....

....

3.NS.1 Make predictions and formulate testable questions. **3.NS.2** Design a fair test. **3.NS.7** Keep accurate records in a notebook during investigations and communicate findings to others using graphs, charts, maps and models through oral and written reports. **3.NS.8** Identify simple patterns in data and propose explanations to account for the patterns. (Also **3.NS.9**)

Design your test.

☐ **4.** Draw how you will set up your test.

☐ **5.** List your steps in the order you will do them.

☐ **6.** Follow the steps you wrote.

☐ **7. Record** your results in the table.

Collect and record your data.

> **Work Like a Scientist**
> It is important to make careful observations. Record all of your observations. Use charts or graphs to help you record.

☐ **8.** After one day, describe your towels in the chart below.

Interpret your data.

☑ **9.** Compare how damp the towels were after one day.

....

....

....

☐ **10.** How does the shape and size of a leaf affect how fast a leaf loses water? Why?

....

....

....

....

☐ **11.** How does a waxy coating help a plant?

....

....

State your conclusion.

12. You conducted an **experiment** to test your **hypothesis.** Compare your hypothesis with your results. **Communicate** your conclusions.

....

....

13. Infer What are 2 adaptations cactuses have that help them survive in the desert?

....

....

Germinating Seeds

Seeds need the right conditions to germinate and grow. Use plastic cups, potting soil, and bean seeds to find out how well seeds germinate and grow with different amounts of water.

- What happened when you watered the seeds too much?
- What happened when you watered the seeds too little?

🔵 3.3.2

Plant Leaves and Food

Plant leaves make food for the plant. Make a card for each material that is used to make food and a card for each material that is produced. Gather all the cards for materials used to make food. Place those cards to your left. Place the cards for the produced materials to your right.

- What do plant leaves use to make food?
- What do plant leaves make?

🔵 3.3.1

Using Scientific Methods

1. Ask a question.
2. State your hypothesis.
3. Identify and control variables.
4. Test your hypothesis.
5. Collect and record your data.
6. Interpret your data.
7. State your conclusion.
8. Go further.

Measurements

Metric and Customary Measurements

The metric system is the measurement system most commonly used in science. Metric units are sometimes called SI units. SI stands for International System. It is called that because these units are used around the world.

These prefixes are used in the metric system:

kilo- means *thousand*
1 kilometer = 1,000 meters

milli- means *one thousandth*
1,000 millimeters = 1 meter or 1 millimeter = 0.001 meter

centi- means *one hundredth*
100 centimeters = 1 meter or 1 centimeter = 0.01 meter

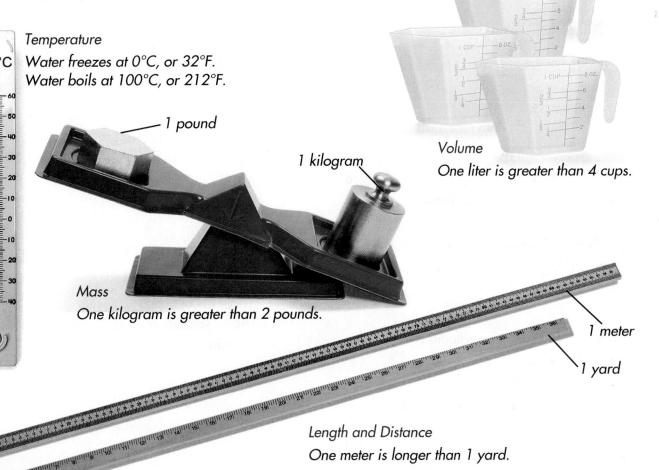

1 liter

1 cup

Volume
One liter is greater than 4 cups.

Temperature
Water freezes at 0°C, or 32°F.
Water boils at 100°C, or 212°F.

1 pound

1 kilogram

Mass
One kilogram is greater than 2 pounds.

1 meter

1 yard

Length and Distance
One meter is longer than 1 yard.

Glossary

The glossary uses letters and signs to show how words are pronounced. The mark ′ is placed after a syllable with a primary or heavy accent. The mark ′ is placed after a syllable with a secondary or lighter accent.

To hear these vocabulary words and definitions, you can refer to the AudioText CD, or log on to the digital path's Vocabulary Smart Cards.

Pronunciation Key

a	in hat	ō	in open	sh	in she
ā	in age	ȯ	in all	th	in thin
â	in care	ô	in order	ŦH	in then
ä	in far	oi	in oil	zh	in measure
e	in let	ou	in out	ə	= a in about
ē	in equal	u	in cup	ə	= e in taken
ėr	in term	u̇	in put	ə	= i in pencil
i	in it	ü	in rule	ə	= o in lemon
ī	in ice	ch	in child	ə	= u in circus
o	in hot	ng	in long		

A

absorb (ab sôrb′) to take in

absorber retener

B

bar graph (bär graf) a graph that helps you compare data and see patterns

gráfica de barras gráfica que ayuda a comparar datos y ver patrones

boil (boil) to change from liquid water into bubbles of water vapor

hervir cambiar de agua en estado líquido a burbujas de vapor

C

carbon dioxide (kär′ bən dī ok′ sīd) a gas in air that is absorbed by some plants

dióxido de carbono gas en el aire que algunas plantas absorben

chart (chärt) a kind of list

tabla tipo de lista

condensation (kon′ den sā′ shən) the change from a gas into a liquid

condensación cambio de estado gaseoso a líquido

design process (di zīn′ pros′ es) a step-by-step method used to solve a problem

proceso de diseño método que se sigue pasos y que se usa para resolver un problema

electrical energy (i lek′ trə kəl en′ ər jē) the movement of electric charges

energía eléctrica el movimiento de cargas eléctricas

energy (en′ ər jē) the ability to do work or to cause change

energía capacidad de hacer trabajo o causar cambios

evaporation (i vap′ ə rā′ shən) the change from liquid water to water vapor

evaporación cambio de agua en estado líquido a vapor

extinct (ek stingkt′) no longer lives on Earth

extinto que ya no existe en la Tierra

fertilizer (fėr′ tl ī′zər) a substance added to soil to help the plant produce more food

fertilzante sustancia que se agrega al suelo para que la planta produzca más alimento

flowering plant (flou′ ər ing plant) a plant with seeds that grows flowers

angiosperma planta con semillas que produce flores

fossil (fos′ əl) remains or mark of a living thing from long ago

fósil restos o marca de un ser vivo que existió hace mucho tiempo

freeze (frēz) to change from a liquid to a solid

congelarse cambiar de líquido a sólido

G

germinate (jèr′ mə nāt) to begin to grow

germinar empezar a crecer

H

hardness (härd′ nis) a description of how firm an object is

dureza descripción de la firmeza de un objeto

I

igneous rock (ig′ nē əs rok) rock that forms when melted rock cools and hardens

roca ígnea roca que se forma cuando las rocas derretidas se enfrian y endurecen

inclined plane (in klīnd′ plān) a slanting surface that connects a lower level to a higher level

plano inclinado superficie inclinada que conecta un nivel bajo con un nivel más alto

inquiry (in kwī′ rē) the process of asking questions

investigación proceso de hacer preguntas

investigate (in ves′ tə gāt) to look for answers

investigar buscar respuestas

K

kinetic energy (ki net′ ik en′ ər jē) energy of motion

energía cinética energía del movimiento

L

lever (lev′ ər) a simple machine to lift and move things by using a stiff bar that rests on a support

palanca máquina simple que se usa para levanter y mover cosas mediante una barra rígida que tiene un punto de apoyo

light energy (līt en′ ər jē) energy we can see

energía luminosa energía que podemos ver

luster (lus′ tər) the way a mineral reflects light

brillo manera en la que un mineral refleja la luz

mass (mas) the amount of matter an object has

masa cantidad de materia que un objeto tiene

matter (mat′ər) anything that takes up space and has mass

materia todo lo que ocupa espacio y tiene masa

mechanical energy (mə kan′ ə kəl en′ ər jē) energy that motion or position gives to an object

energía mecánica energía que un objeto obtiene por su posición o desplazamiento

melt (melt) to change from a solid to a liquid

derretirse cambiar de sólido a líquido

metamorphic rock (met′ ə môr′ fik rok) rock that forms when existing rock is changed by heat and pressure

roca metamórfica roca que se forma cuando las rocas existentes cambian debido al calor y la presión

mineral (min′ ər əl) natural, nonliving material that makes up rocks

mineral material natural y sin vida del que están formadas las rocas

model (mod′ l) a copy of something

modelo copia de algo

natural resource (nach′ ər əl rē′ sôrs) an important material from Earth that living things need

recurso natural un material importante de la Tierra que los seres vivos necesitan

nonrenewable resource (non′ ri nü′ ə bəl rē′ sôrs) resource that cannot be replaced once it is used up

recurso no renovable recurso que no se puede reemplazar cuando se acaba

nutrient (nü′ trē ənt) any material needed by living things for energy, growth, and repair

nutriente cualquier sustancia que los seres vivos necesitan para obtener energía, crecer y reponerse

oxygen (ok′ sə jən) a gas in the air that plants and animals need to live

oxígeno gas en el aire que las plantas y los animals necesitan para vivir

pitch (pich) how high or low a sound is

tono cuán agudo o grave es un sonido

pollinate (pol′ ə nāt) to carry pollen to

polinizar llevar polen de un lugar a otro

potential energy (pə ten′ shəl en′ ər jē) stored energy

energía potencial energía almacenada

procedure (prə sē′ jər) plan for testing a hypothesis

procedimiento plan que se usa para poner a prueba una hipótesis

property (prop′ ər tē) something about matter that you can observe with one or more of your senses

propiedad algo en la materia que puedes percibir con uno o más de tus sentidos

prototype (prō′ tə tīp) the first working product that uses a design

prototipo el primer producto que funciona y que sique un diseño

pulley (pùl′ ē) a machine that changes the direction of motion of an object to which a force is applied

polea máquina que cambia la dirección en que se mueve un objeto al que se ha aplicado fuerza

reflect (ri flekt′) to bounce off

reflejar hacer rebotar algo

---

refract (ri frakt′) to bend

refractor desviar o inclinar

---

renewable resource (ri nü′ ə bəl rē′ sôrs) resource that can be replaced in a fairly short time

recurso renovable recurso que se puede reemplazar en poco tiempo

---

reproduce (rē′ prə düs′) to make more of the same kind

reproducir hacer más de una misma cosa

research (ri sėrch′) to look for facts about something

hacer una investigación buscar datos sobre algo

---

rock (rok) natural, solid, nonliving material made from one or more minerals

roca material natural, sólido sin vida, compuesto por uno o más minerales

scientist (sī′ ən tist) person who asks questions about the natural world

científico persona cuyo trabajo implica hacer preguntas sobre el mundo y la naturaleza

---

screw (skrü) an inclined plane wrapped around a center post

tornillo plano inclinado enrollado alrededor de un eje central

---

sedimentary rock (sed′ ə men′ tər ē rok) rock that forms when sediments are pressed together and cemented

roca sedimentaria roca que se forma por la acumulación de sedimentos unidos a gran presión

shadow (shad′ ō) a dark area made when an object blocks light between a light source and a surface

sombra región oscura que se produce cuando un objeto colocado entre una fuente de luz y una superficie bloquea la luz

sieve (siv) a tool used for separating materials

criba instrumento que se usa para separar materiales

silt (silt) very fine particles of earth and sand carried by moving water

limo partículas muy finas de tierra y arena que son arrastradas por el agua en movimiento

sound energy (sound en′ ər jē) energy we can hear

energía sonora energía que podemos oír

spore (spôr) a small cell that grows into a new plant

spora célula pequeña que se convierte en una planta nueva

states of matter (stāts uv mat′ ər) forms that matter can take

estados de la materia formas que la materia puede tener

streak (strēk) the color of the powder that a mineral leaves when it is rubbed across a rough surface

raya color del polvo que un mineral deja cuando se lo frota contra una superficie rugosa

T

technology (tek nol′ ə jē) use of science knowledge to invent tools and new ways of doing things

tecnología uso del conocimiento científico para inventar instrumentos y nuevas maneras nuevas de hacer las cosas

texture (teks′ chər) how an object feels to the touch

textura cómo se siente un objeto al tocarlo

tool (tül) object used to do work

instrumento objeto que se usa para trabajar

unit of measure (yü′ nit uv mezh′ ər) quantity you use to measure

unidad de medida cantidad que usa para medir

vibration (vī brā′ shən) a quick back and forth movement

vibración movimiento rápido hacia delante y hacia atrás

volume (vol′ yəm) amount of space matter takes up

volumen cantidad de espacio que ocupa la materia

volume (vol′ yəm) how loud or soft a sound is

volumen cuán fuerte o suave es un sonido

wave (wāv) a disturbance that carries energy from one point to another point

onda perturbación que lleva energía de un punto a otro

wedge (wej) two slanted sides that end in a sharp edge

cuña dos lados inclinados que terminan con un borde filoso

wheel and axle (wēl and ak′ səl) a round wheel attached to a post

eje y rueda figura circular que gira alrededor de una varilla

work (wėrk) to use force to move an object across a distance

trabajo uso de una fuerza para mover un objeto, por cierta distancia

Index

This index lists the pages on which a topic appears. Page numbers following a *p* refer to a photograph or illustration. Page numbers following a *c* refer to a chart or graph.

Credits

Staff Credits

The people who made up the *Interactive Science* team — representing composition services, core design digital and multimedia production services, digital product development, editorial, editorial services, manufacturing, and production — are listed below.

Geri Amani, Alisa Anderson, Jose Arrendondo, Amy Austin, Scott Baker, Lindsay Bellino, Charlie Bink, Bridget Binstock, Holly Blessen, Robin Bobo, Craig Bottomley, Jim Brady, Laura Brancky, Chris Budzisz, Mary Chingwa, Sitha Chhor, Caroline Chung, Margaret Clampitt, Kier Cline, Brandon Cole, Mitch Coulter, AnnMarie Coyne, Fran Curran, Dana Damiano, Nancy Duffner, Amanda Ferguson, David Gall, Mark Geyer, Amy Goodwin, Gerardine Griffin, Chris Haggerty, Laura Hancko, Jericho Hernandez, Autumn Hickenlooper, Guy Huff, George Jacobson, Marian Jones, Kathi Kalina, Chris Kammer, Sheila Kanitsch, Alyse Kondrat, Mary Kramer, Thea Limpus, Dominique Mariano, Lori McGuire, Melinda Medina, Angelina Mendez, Claudi Mimo, John Moore, Phoebe Novak, Anthony Nuccio, Jeffrey Osier, Julianne Regnier, Charlene Rimsa, Rebecca Roberts, Camille Salerno, Manuel Sanchez, Carol Schmitz, Amanda Seldera, Sheetal Shah, Jeannine Shelton El, Geri Shulman, Greg Sorenson, Samantha Sparkman, Mindy Spelius, Karen Stockwell, Dee Sunday, Dennis Tarwood, Jennie Teece, Lois Teesdale, Michaela Tudela, Oscar Vera, Dave Wade, Tom Wickland, James Yagelski, Tim Yetzina, Diane Zimmermann

Illustrations

116 Jeff Grunewald; 193, 218 Big Sesh Studios; 226 Precision Graphics; 232, 243 Alan Barnard; S0343 Cora Sue Nicholas. All other illustrations Chandler Digital Art

Photographs

Every effort has been made to secure permission and provide appropriate credit for photographic material. The publisher deeply regrets any omission and pledges to correct errors called to its attention in subsequent editions.

Unless otherwise acknowledged, all photographs are the property of Pearson Education, Inc.

Photo locators denoted as follows: Top (T), Center (C), Bottom (B), Left (L), Right (R), Background (Bkgd)

COVER: ©All Canada Photos/SuperStock

2 ©Kim Karpeles/Alamy Images; 6 (T) ©gary corbett/Alamy Images, (C) Florida Division of Forestry, Tallahassee; 7 (CR) ©Doug Steley A/Alamy Images; 9 (TR) ©Will & Deni McIntyre/Photo Researchers, Inc.; 10 (T) ©Dennis Hallinan/Alamy Images; 11 (B) ©dmac/Alamy Images; 12 (T) ©forestpath/Shutterstock; 13 (CR) ©matthiasengelien/Alamy; 15 (TR) ©Jeff Greenberg/Alamy Images; 16 (T) ©Science Source/Photo Researchers, Inc.; 17 (BR) ©Aaron Haupt/Photo Researchers, Inc.; 20 (TL) ©Alfred Pasieka/Photo Researchers, Inc.; 22 (T) ©Images & Stories/Alamy Images; 23 (T) ©Chris Johnson/Alamy Images, (B) ©Images & Stories/Alamy; 26 (T) ©Ariel Skelley/Blend/Jupiter Images; 28 (TR) ©Rob Walls/Alamy Images; 29 (BR) ©Bob Daemmrich/PhotoEdit, Inc., (TL) ©Jubal Harshaw/Shutterstock; 32 (B) ©Andy Crawford/DK Images; 33 (TR) ©imagebroker/Alamy Images; 34 (T) ©Idealink Photography/Alamy; 35 (CR) Getty Images; 36 (BL) ©Monkey Business Images/Shutterstock, (CL) Jupiter Images; 37 (TR) ©Andrey Burmakin/Shutterstock; 40 B. Tristan Denyer; 41 (CR) ©Doug Steley A/Alamy Images, (TC) ©forestpath/Shutterstock, (TR) ©Will & Deni McIntyre/Photo Researchers, Inc.; 43 (BR) ©Bob Daemmrich/PhotoEdit, Inc., (CC) Getty Images; 45 (TL) ©Dennis Hallinan/Alamy Images, (TL) ©gary corbett/Alamy Images, (CL) ©Images & Stories/Alamy Images, (BL) ©Jubal Harshaw/Shutterstock, (BL) Jupiter Images; 49 (TC) ©Holmberg/Sipa/NewsCom, (L) Mari Tefre/Svalbard Global Seed Vault/Courtesy, Ministry of Agriculture and Food, Oslo, Norway; 50 ©ImageState/Alamy Images; 53 (R) ©Bronwyn Photo/Shutterstock; 54 (T) ©Tony Freeman/PhotoEdit, (BL) Getty Images, (BC) Manuel Sanchez; 55 (BR) Getty Images, (CR) Jupiter Images; 56 (B) ©Pinchuk Alexey/Shutterstock; 57 (CR) Getty Images, (TL) Jupiter Images; 58 (T) ©Stockbyte/Getty Images; 59 (BC) Stockdisc; 60 ©Tom Silver/Corbis; 68 (B) ©Phase4Photography/Shutterstock; 72 (R) ©PhotoAlto/SuperStock, (TR) Jupiter Images; 73 (BR) ©Pinchuk Alexey/Shutterstock, (CC) ©Stockbyte/Getty Images, (CR) Getty Images, (TR, TC) Jupiter Images; 77 (B) ©ImageState/Alamy Images, (CL) ©Tom Silver/Corbis, (TL) Jupiter Images; 78 (CL) Getty Images, (CC) Jupiter Images; 81 ©Thien Eu/Shutterstock, (BL) Stockdisc; 82 ©UpperCut Images/SuperStock; 85 ©DK Images; 86 (T) ©Lisa Lehmann/Lisa Lehmann Photo Art & Design; 87 (CR) Photos to Go/Photolibrary; 90 (B) Image100; 91 (TL) Image100; 93 (BR) Gary Ombler/Courtesy John Rigg, The Robot Hut/©DK Images; 94 (B) ©Stone/Getty Images; 95 (CR) ©James Steidl/Shutterstock; 96 ©@erics/Shutterstock; 97 (CR) ©Tom Szuba/Masterfile Corporation; 98 (T) ©yuyangc/Shutterstock; 99 (B) ©Zhiltsov Alexandr/Shutterstock; 100 (TL) ©Sascha Burkard/Shutterstock, (BR) ©Tomislav Forgo/Shutterstock; 101 Getty Images; 102 ©Craig Tuttle/Corbis, (C, B) Getty Images; 104 (B) ©Pierre Arsenault/Masterfile Corporation; 105 (TR, TL, TC) Getty Images; 106 (T) Getty Images; 108 (BL) ©Datacraft - Hana/Alamy; 109 (TR) ©Christophe Testi/Shutterstock; 110 (TL) ©Marcia Griffen/Animals Animals/Earth Scenes, (BL) Getty Images; 111 (TR) ©Robert Ginn/PhotoEdit, Inc.; 112 (T) ©Natural Selection/Jupiter Images; 113 (BR) ©Image Source ; 116 (TL) ©Planner/Shutterstock; 120 (R) NASA; 121 (CC, BC) Image100, (TR) Photos to Go/Photolibrary; 123 (BC) ©Christophe Testi/Shutterstock, (TL) ©Marcia Griffen/Animals Animals/Earth Scenes, (CC) ©Pierre Arsenault/Masterfile Corporation, (BR) ©Sascha Burkard/Shutterstock, (CR) ©Zhiltsov Alexandr/Shutterstock, (TC) Getty Images; 125 (CL) ©Datacraft - Hana/Alamy, (TL) ©James Steidl/Shutterstock, (BL) ©Natural Selection/Jupiter Images, (CL) ©Pierre Arsenault/Masterfile Corporation, (BC) ©UpperCut Images/SuperStock, (TL) Photos to Go/Photolibrary; 126 (TL, CL) Image100; 129 ©Doug James/Shutterstock; 130 ©Mark Lewis/Getty Images; 133 (B) ©MatthiolaC/Alamy; 134 (B) ©Brent Walker/Shutterstock, (CR) ©Photo Researchers/Alamy; 135 (CR) ©Stock Connection Blue

This is your book.

You can write in it.

Take Note

This space is yours. It is great for drawing diagrams and making notes.

This is your book.

You can write in it.

This is your book.

You can write in it.

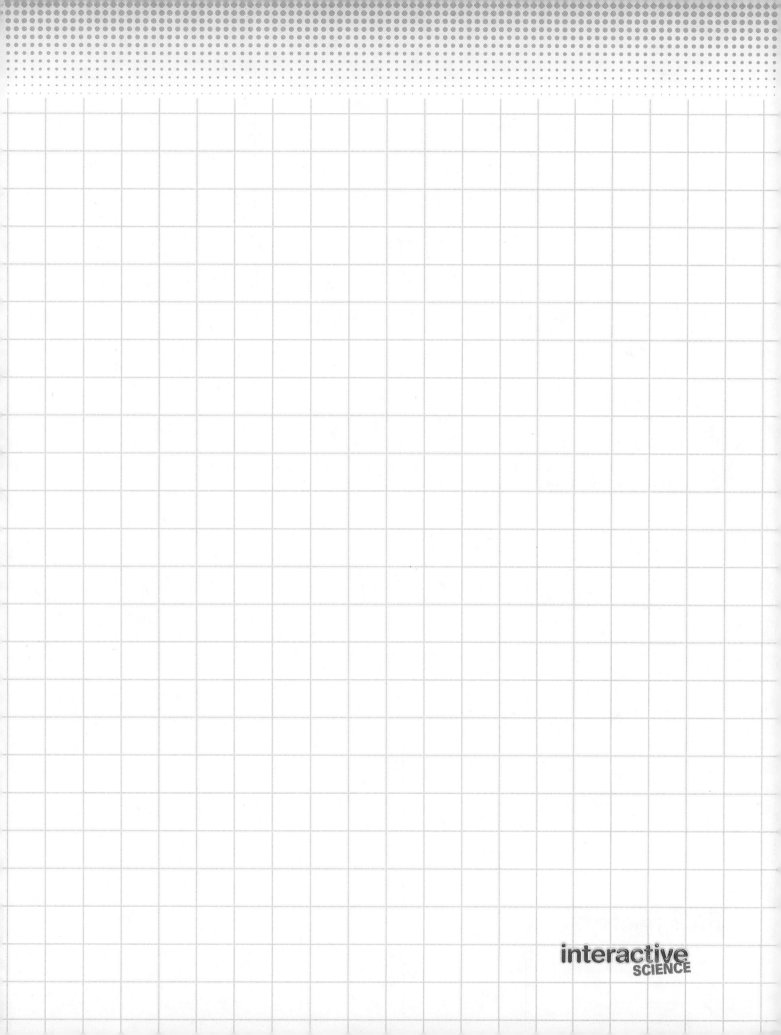

interactive
SCIENCE

This is your book.

You can write in it.